From the Heart

quilts to cherish

Compiled by Dawn Anderson

Martingale™
& COMPANY

Credits

President	Nancy J. Martin
CEO	Daniel J. Martin
Publisher	Jane Hamada
Editorial Director	Mary V. Green
Managing Editor	Tina Cook
Technical Editor	Dawn Anderson
Copy Editor	Allison A. Merrill
Design Director	Stan Green
Illustrator	Laurel Strand
Cover Designer	Stan Green
Text Designer	Trina Stahl
Photographer	Brent Kane

That Patchwork Place® is an imprint of Martingale & Company™.

From the Heart: Quilts to Cherish
© 2002 by Martingale & Company

Martingale & Company
20205 144th Avenue NE
Woodinville, WA 98072-8478 USA
www.martingale-pub.com

Printed in Hong Kong
07 06 05 04 03 02   8 7 6 5 4 3 2 1

The information in this book is presented in good faith, but no warranty is given nor results guaranteed. Since Martingale & Company has no control over choice of materials or procedures, the company assumes no responsibility for the use of this information.

Library of Congress Cataloging-in-Publication Data

From the heart : quilts to cherish / compiled by Dawn Anderson.
     p.   cm.
   ISBN 1-56477-415-5
   1. Quilting—Patterns.   2. Patchwork—Patterns.
   3. Heart in art.   I. Anderson, Dawn.
TT835 .F758 2002
746.46'041—dc21
                                        2001051418

Contents

Introduction · 4

Quiltmaking Basics · 5

Fabrics · 5
Supplies · 5
Rotary Cutting · 6
Machine Piecing · 7
Pressing · 7
Basic Appliqué · 8
Assembling the Quilt Top · 9
Adding Borders · 10
Preparing to Quilt · 12
Quilting Techniques · 13
Finishing · 14
Embroidery Stitches · 17

Little Sweethearts · 18

Hip Cats · 22

Quilts Bring Hearts
    Together · 31

Summer of the Hearts · 37

Thirties Hearts
    and Arrows · 48

Summer Hearts · 52

Lots of Luvs · 58

Petit-Four Hearts · 63

Patchwork Hearts · 67

Soft Summer Roses · 70

A Blue and Yellow
    Basket · 73

Introduction

IT IS REMARKABLE how the simple heart shape—two gentle curves that meet in a single point—has become a symbol for so many sentiments. It has been used to express friendship, compassion, devotion, fondness, courage, and kindness. It can cheer, comfort, console, inspire, and raise someone's spirits.

Of course, the heart is most commonly used as a romantic symbol: to melt someone's heart. It can communicate tender feelings without a word, honor a love that has endured over the years, even help heal a broken heart. Hearts abound on Valentine's Day, but the heart is not bound by any holiday. And just as a heart can express any loving emotion, the designs in *From the Heart* will help you stitch a quilt appropriate to any heartfelt occasion.

The contributors to this book created these heart-filled quilts with someone they love in mind. Small, simple projects include Sandy Bonsib's "Patchwork Hearts" (page 67), a fun project featuring pieced hearts appliquéd to a background fabric and framed with bold borders. Cleo Nollette's "Soft Summer Roses" (page 70) uses just one background fabric to frame eighteen scrappy, hand-appliquéd hearts. Either quilt is a

perfect quick gift to send friendly feelings along to its recipient.

For a larger quilt, try "Summer Hearts" from Beth Merrill Kovich (page 52). Beth uses cheerful thirties reproduction fabrics in pieced, on-point hearts framed by a beautiful Fan-block border. Karen Walker's kaleidoscopic "Summer of the Hearts" (page 37) uses straight-line piecing to create the illusion of curved heart tops. And Janet Carija Brandt's "Petit-Four Hearts" (page 63) combines wool-felt appliqué with easy embroidered accents.

Looking for a gift for a fellow quilter? "Quilts Bring Hearts Together" (page 31), made by Bridget Haugh, is a welcoming wall hanging that sounds a simple and true embroidered message. A lively border of traditional squares, diamonds, and pinwheels completes a fine gift to celebrate friendship between quilters.

Whether you want to thank a loved one, encourage a friend, cheer someone close to you, or simply say "I love you," you will find a quilt to express your warmest feelings in this book. So, visit your local quilt shop, dig through your stash, and start stitching a quilt today that is truly "from the heart."

Quiltmaking Basics

Fabrics

FOR BEST RESULTS, select high-quality, 100 percent–cotton fabrics. All-cotton fabrics hold their shape well and are easy to handle. Cotton blends can be more difficult to stitch and press. Sometimes, however, a cotton blend is worth a little extra effort if it is the perfect fabric for your quilt.

Yardage requirements for all the projects in this book are based on 42" of usable fabric after prewashing. Some quilts call for an assortment of scraps. If you have access to scraps, feel free to use them and purchase only those fabrics you need to complete the quilt you are making.

Prewash all fabric to preshrink, test for colorfastness, and remove excess dye. Wash dark and light colors separately so that dark colors do not run onto light fabrics. Some fabrics may require several rinses to eliminate the excess dyes. Press the fabric so you can cut out the pieces accurately.

Supplies

Sewing machine: To machine piece, you'll need a sewing machine that has a good straight stitch. You'll also need a walking foot or darning foot if you are going to machine quilt.

Rotary-cutting tools: You will need a rotary cutter, cutting mat, and clear acrylic rulers in a variety of sizes, including 6" x 6", 6" x 24", 12" x 12", and 15" x 15".

Thread: Use a good-quality, all-purpose cotton or cotton-covered polyester thread.

Needles: For machine piecing, a size 70/10 or 80/12 works well for most cottons. For hand appliqué, choose a needle that will glide easily through the edges of the appliqué pieces. Size 10 (fine) to size 12 (very fine) needles work well.

Pins: Long, fine "quilter's" pins with glass or plastic heads are easy to handle. Small ½" to ¾" sequin pins work well for appliqué.

Scissors: Use your best scissors to cut fabric only. Use an older pair of scissors to cut paper, cardboard, and template plastic. Small 4" scissors are handy for clipping threads.

Sandpaper board: This is an invaluable tool for marking fabric accurately. You can easily make one by adhering very fine sandpaper to a hard surface, such as wood, cardboard, poster board, or needlework mounting board. The sandpaper grabs the fabric and keeps it from slipping as you mark.

Template plastic: Use clear or frosted plastic (available at quilt shops) to make durable, accurate templates.

Seam ripper: Use this tool to remove stitches sewn incorrectly.

Marking tools: A variety of tools are available to mark fabrics when tracing around templates or marking quilting lines. Use a sharp #2 pencil or fine-lead mechanical pencil on light-colored fabrics; use a white or yellow marking pencil on dark fabrics. Chalk pencils or chalk-wheel markers also make clear marks on fabric. Test your marking tool to make sure you can remove its marks easily.

Rotary Cutting

THE PROJECTS IN this book include instructions for quick-and-easy rotary cutting wherever possible. All measurements include standard ¼"-wide seam allowances, unless otherwise indicated. For those unfamiliar with rotary cutting, a brief introduction is provided below. For more detailed information, see Donna Lynn Thomas's *Shortcuts: A Concise Guide to Rotary Cutting* (Martingale & Company, 1999).

1. Fold the fabric and match selvages, aligning the crosswise and lengthwise grains as much as possible. Place the folded edge closest to you on the cutting mat. Align a square ruler along the folded edge of the fabric; then place a long, straight ruler to the left of the square ruler, just covering the uneven raw edges on the left side of the fabric.

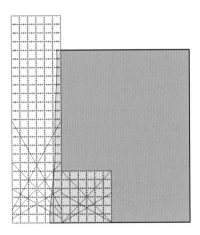

Remove the square ruler and cut along the right edge of the long ruler, rolling the rotary cutter away from you. Discard this strip. (Reverse this procedure if you are left-handed.)

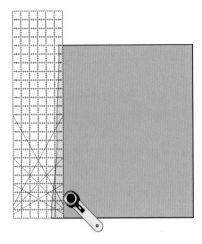

2. To cut strips, align the required measurement on the ruler with the newly cut edge of the fabric. For example, to cut a 3"-wide strip, place the 3" ruler mark on the edge of the fabric.

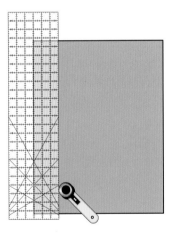

3. To cut squares, cut strips in the required widths. Trim away the selvage ends of the strip. Align the required measurement on the ruler with the left edge of the strip and cut a square. Continue cutting squares until you have the number needed.

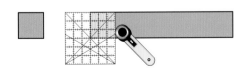

Machine Piecing

Sewing Accurate Seam Allowances

FOR MACHINE piecing, it is important to maintain a consistent ¼"-wide seam allowance. Otherwise, the quilt blocks will not be the desired finished size, which in turn affects the size of everything else in the quilt, including alternate blocks, sashings, and borders. Measurements for all components for each quilt are based on blocks that finish accurately to the desired size plus ¼" on each edge for seam allowances.

Establish an exact ¼"-wide seam guide on your machine. Some machines have a special foot that measures exactly ¼" from the center needle position to the edge of the foot. This feature allows you to use the edge of the presser foot to guide the fabric for a perfect ¼"-wide seam allowance. If your machine doesn't have such a foot, create a seam guide by placing the edge of a piece of tape or moleskin ¼" from the needle.

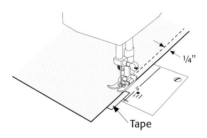

Chain Piecing

CHAIN PIECING is an efficient system that saves time.

1. Sew the first pair of pieces from cut edge to cut edge, using 12 stitches per inch. At the end of the seam, stop sewing, but do not cut the thread.

2. Feed the next pair of pieces under the presser foot, as close as possible to the first pair. Continue feeding pieces through the machine without cutting the threads in between. There is no need to backstitch, since each seam will be crossed and held by another seam.

3. When all pieces have been sewn, remove the chain from the machine and clip the threads between the pieces.

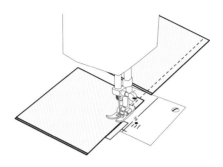

Easing

IF TWO pieces that will be sewn together are slightly different in size (less than ⅛"), pin the places where the two pieces should match and in the middle, if necessary, to distribute the excess fabric evenly. Sew the seam with the longer piece on the bottom. The feed dogs will ease the two pieces together.

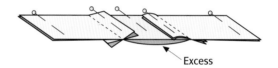

Pressing

THE TRADITIONAL RULE in quiltmaking is to press seams to one side, toward the darker color wherever possible. Individual project instructions may specify how you should press seams, or arrows may be included in illustrations. Press the seam flat from the wrong side first, then press the seam in the desired direction from the right side. Press carefully to avoid distorting the shapes.

When joining two seamed units, plan ahead and press the seam allowances in opposite directions as shown to reduce bulk and make it easier to match seam lines. Where two seams meet, the seam allowances will butt against each other, making it easier to join units with perfectly matched seam intersections.

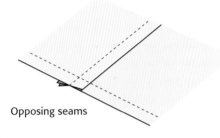

Opposing seams

Basic Appliqué

INSTRUCTIONS ARE PROVIDED for needle-turn appliqué. Use another method if you prefer.

Making Templates

MAKE YOUR appliqué templates from clear or frosted plastic because they will be more durable and accurate than templates made from cardboard. Since you can see through the plastic, it is easy to trace the templates accurately.

Place template plastic over each pattern and trace with a fine-line permanent marker. Do not add seam allowances. Cut out the templates on the drawn lines. Mark the pattern name and grain-line arrow (if applicable) on the template.

Needle-Turn Appliqué

1. Using a plastic template, mark the design on the right side of the appliqué fabric. Use a #2 pencil on light fabrics, a white or yellow pencil on dark fabrics.

2. Cut out the fabric piece, adding a scant ¼"-wide seam allowance all around.

3. Position the appliqué piece on the background fabric; pin or baste in place.

4. Starting on a straight edge, use the tip of the needle to gently turn under the seam allowance, about ½" at a time. Hold the turned seam allowance firmly between the thumb and first finger of your left hand (reverse if left-handed) as you stitch the appliqué to the background. Use a longer needle—a Sharp or Milliner's needle—to help you control the seam allowance and turn it under neatly. Use the traditional appliqué stitch (see section below).

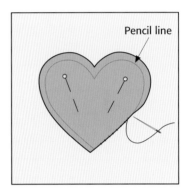

Pencil line

Traditional Appliqué Stitch

THE TRADITIONAL appliqué stitch or blind stitch is appropriate for sewing all appliqué shapes, including sharp points and curves.

1. Tie a knot in a single strand of thread approximately 18" long.

2. Hide the knot by slipping the needle into the seam allowance from the wrong side of the appliqué piece, bringing it out on the fold line.

3. Work from right to left if you are right-handed, or left to right if you are left-handed. Start the first stitch by moving the needle straight off the appliqué, inserting the needle into the background fabric. Let the needle travel under the background fabric, parallel to the edge of the appliqué, bringing it up about ⅛" away, along the pattern line.

4. As you bring the needle up, pierce the edge of the appliqué piece, catching only 1 or 2 threads of the folded edge.

5. Move the needle straight off the appliqué into the background fabric. Let your needle travel under the background, bringing it up about ⅛" away, again catching the edge of the appliqué.

6. Give the thread a slight tug and continue stitching.

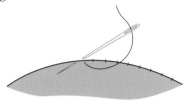

Appliqué stitch

7. To end your stitching, pull the needle through to the wrong side. Behind the appliqué piece, take 2 small stitches, making knots by taking your needle through the loops. Check the right side to see if the thread "shadows" through your background. If it does, take 1 more small stitch on the wrong side to direct the tail of the thread under the appliqué fabric.

8. If desired, trim the background fabric that lies under each appliqué piece to reduce the bulk and make it easier to quilt. Turn the block over and make a tiny cut in the background fabric. Trim the fabric ¼" away from the stitching line, being careful not to cut through the appliquéd piece.

Assembling the Quilt Top

Squaring Up Blocks

AFTER STITCHING your quilt blocks together, take the time to square them up. Use a large, square ruler to measure your blocks and make sure they are the desired size plus an extra ¼" on each edge for seam allowances. For example, if you are making 6" blocks, they should all measure 6½" before you sew them together. If your blocks vary slightly in size, trim the larger blocks to match the size of the smallest one. Be sure to trim all four sides; otherwise, your block will be lopsided.

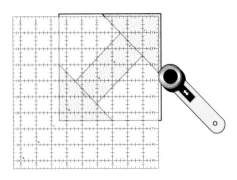

If your blocks are not the required finished size, you will have to adjust all the other components of the quilt accordingly.

Making Straight-Set Quilts

1. Arrange the blocks as shown in the diagram provided with each quilt.

2. Sew the blocks together in horizontal rows; press the seams in opposite directions from row to row (unless directed otherwise).

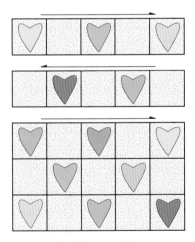

Straight-set quilts

3. Sew the rows together, making sure to match the seams between the blocks.

Making Diagonally Set Quilts

1. Arrange the blocks, side setting triangles, and corner setting triangles as shown in the diagram provided with each quilt.

2. Sew the blocks together in diagonal rows; press the seams in opposite directions from row to row (unless directed otherwise).

3. Sew the rows together, making sure to match the seams between the blocks. Sew on the corner setting triangles last.

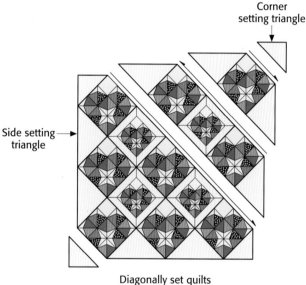

Diagonally set quilts

NOTE: *Sometimes side and corner setting triangles are cut larger than necessary and trimmed later.*

Adding Borders

FOR BEST RESULTS, do not cut border strips and sew them directly to the quilt top without measuring first. Often, a quilt measures slightly more at its edges than through its center, due to stretching during construction. Measure the quilt top through the center in both directions to determine how long to cut the border strips. This step ensures that the finished quilt will be as straight and "square" as possible, without wavy edges.

Plain borders are commonly cut along the crosswise grain and seamed where extra length is needed. Borders cut from the lengthwise grain of fabric require extra yardage, but seaming to achieve the required length is then unnecessary.

Straight-Cut Borders

1. Measure the length of the quilt top through the center. Cut border strips to that measurement, piecing as necessary. Mark the centers of the quilt edges and the border strips. Pin the borders to the sides of the quilt top, matching the center marks and ends and easing as necessary. Sew the border strips in place. Press seams toward the borders.

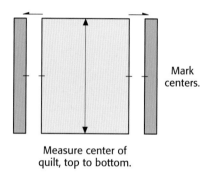

Mark centers.

Measure center of quilt, top to bottom.

2. Measure the width of the quilt top through the center, including the side borders just added. Cut border strips to that measurement, piecing as necessary. Mark the centers of the quilt edges and the border strips. Pin the borders to the top and bottom edges of the quilt top, matching the center marks and ends and easing as necessary; stitch. Press seams toward the borders.

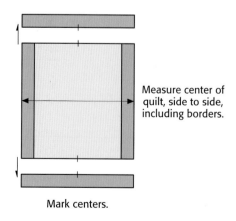

Measure center of quilt, side to side, including borders.

Mark centers.

Borders with Corner Squares

1. Measure the width and length of the quilt top through the center. Cut border strips to those measurements, piecing as necessary.

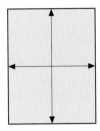

2. Mark the centers of the quilt edges and the border strips. Pin the side border strips to opposite sides of the quilt top, matching centers and ends, and easing as necessary. Sew the side border strips; press seams toward the borders.

3. Cut corner squares the required size (the cut width of the border strips). Sew one corner square to each end of the remaining two border strips; press seams toward the border strips. Pin the border strips to the top and bottom edges of the quilt top. Match centers, seams between the border strips and corner squares, and ends, easing as necessary; stitch. Press seams toward the borders.

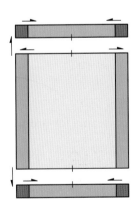

Borders with Mitered Corners

1. Estimate the finished outside dimensions of your quilt, including borders. Border strips should be cut to this length plus at least ½" for seam allowances; it's safer to add 3" to 4" to give yourself some leeway (piece border strips as necessary to achieve the desired length). For example, if your quilt top measures 35½" x 50½" across the center and you want a 5"-wide finished border, your quilt will measure 45" x 60" after borders are attached.

NOTE: *If your quilt has multiple borders, sew the individual strips together and treat the resulting unit as a single border strip.*

2. Fold the quilt in half and mark the centers of the quilt edges. Fold each border strip in half and mark the center with a pin.

3. Measure the length and width of the quilt top across the center. Note the measurements.

4. Place a pin at each end of the side border strips to mark the length of the quilt top. Repeat with the top and bottom borders.

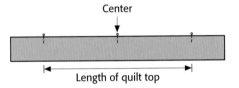

Center

Length of quilt top

5. Pin the borders to the quilt top, matching the centers. Line up the pins at each end of the border strip with the edges of the quilt. Stitch, beginning and ending the stitching ¼" from the raw edges of the quilt top. Repeat with the remaining borders.

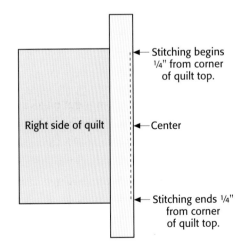

Stitching begins ¼" from corner of quilt top.

Right side of quilt

Center

Stitching ends ¼" from corner of quilt top.

6. Lay the first corner to be mitered on the ironing board. Fold under one border strip at a 45° angle to the other strip. Press and pin.

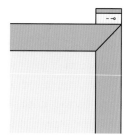

7. Fold the quilt with right sides together, lining up the edges of the border. If necessary, use a ruler to draw a pencil line on the crease to make the line more visible. Stitch on the crease, sewing from the corner to the outside edges.

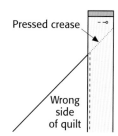

Pressed crease

Wrong side of quilt

8. Press the seam open and trim away excess border strips, leaving a ¼"-wide seam allowance.

9. Repeat with the remaining corners.

Preparing to Quilt

Marking the Quilting Lines

WHETHER YOU SHOULD mark the quilting design or not depends upon the type of quilting you will be doing. Marking is not necessary if you plan to quilt in the ditch, outline-quilt a uniform distance from seam lines, or free-motion quilt in a random pattern. For more complex quilting designs, mark the quilt top before the quilt is layered with batting and backing.

Choose a marking tool that will be visible on your fabric, and test it on fabric scraps to make sure the marks can be removed easily. See "Marking Tools" on page 5 for options. Masking tape can also be used to mark straight quilting. Tape only small sections at a time and remove the tape when you stop at the end of the day; otherwise, the sticky residue may be difficult to remove from the fabric.

Layering the Quilt

THE QUILT "sandwich" consists of the backing, batting, and quilt top. Cut the quilt backing at least 4" larger than the quilt top all the way around. For large quilts, it is usually necessary to sew two or three lengths of fabric together either lengthwise or crosswise to make a backing the required size. Trim away the selvages before piecing the lengths together. Press the backing seams open to make quilting easier.

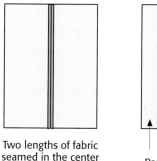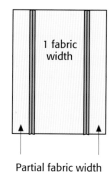

1 fabric width

Two lengths of fabric seamed in the center

Partial fabric width

Batting comes packaged in standard bed sizes, or it can be purchased by the yard. Several weights and thicknesses are available. Thick battings are fine for tied quilts and comforters; a thinner batting is better, however, if you intend to quilt by hand or machine.

To put it all together:

1. Spread the backing, wrong side up, on a flat, clean surface. Anchor it with pins or masking tape. Be careful not to stretch the backing out of shape.

2. Spread the batting over the backing, smoothing out any wrinkles.

3. Place the pressed quilt top, right side up, on top of the batting. Smooth out any wrinkles and make sure the edges of the quilt top are parallel to the edges of the backing.

4. Starting in the center, baste with needle and thread and work diagonally to each corner.

Continue basting in a grid of horizontal and vertical lines 6" to 8" apart. Finish by basting around the edges.

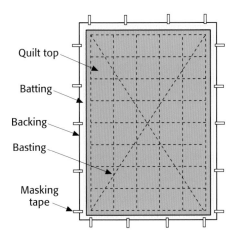

NOTE: *For machine quilting, you may baste the layers with #2 rustproof safety pins. Place pins about 6" to 8" apart, away from areas you intend to quilt.*

Quilting Techniques

Hand Quilting

TO QUILT by hand, you will need short, sturdy needles (called Betweens), quilting thread, and a thimble to fit the middle finger of your sewing hand. Most quilters also use a frame or hoop to support their work. Use the smallest needle you can comfortably handle; the finer the needle, the smaller your stitches will be.

1. Thread your needle with a single strand of quilting thread about 18" long; make a small knot. Insert the needle in the top layer about 1" from the place where you want to start stitching. Pull the needle out at the point where quilting will begin and gently pull the thread until the knot pops through the top of the fabric and into the batting.

2. Take small, evenly spaced stitches through all 3 quilt layers.

3. Rock the needle up and down through all layers, until you have 3 or 4 stitches on the needle. Place your other hand underneath the quilt so you can feel the needle point with the tip of your finger when a stitch is taken.

4. To end a line of quilting, make a small knot close to the last stitch; then backstitch, running the thread a needle's length through the batting. Gently pull the thread until the knot pops into the batting; clip the thread at the quilt's surface.

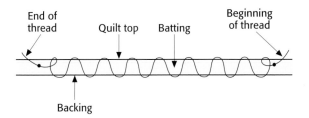

Machine Quilting

MACHINE QUILTING takes much less time than hand quilting and is suitable for all types of quilts, from small wall hangings to bed quilts. For straight-line quilting, such as quilting in the ditch or outline quilting, it is extremely helpful to have a walking foot to help feed the quilt layers through the machine without shifting or puckering. Some machines have a built-in walking foot; other machines require a separate attachment.

Walking foot

 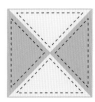

Quilting in the ditch   Outline quilting

For free-motion quilting, you need a darning foot and the ability to drop the feed dogs on your machine. With free-motion quilting, you do not turn the fabric under the needle but instead guide the fabric in the direction of the design. Use free-motion quilting to outline-quilt a pattern in the fabric or to create stippling and many other curved designs.

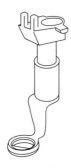

Darning foot

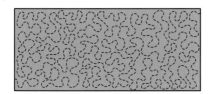

Free-motion quilting

Finishing

Straight-Grain Binding

FOR A French double-fold binding, cut strips to the width indicated for each project, or 2" wide. Cut strips across the width of the fabric. You will need enough strips to go around the perimeter of the quilt plus 10" for seams and mitered corners.

1. Sew strips end to end, right sides together, to make one long piece of binding. Join strips at right angles and stitch across the corner as shown. Trim excess fabric and press the seams open.

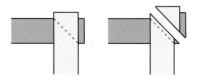

2. Fold the strip in half lengthwise, wrong sides together, and press. Turn under ¼" at a 45° angle at one end of the strip and press. Turning the end under at an angle distributes the bulk so you won't have a lump where the two ends of the binding meet.

Fold line

3. Trim the batting and backing even with the quilt top. If you plan to add a hanging sleeve, do so now, before attaching the binding (see page 16).

4. Starting on one side of the quilt and using a ¼"-wide seam allowance, stitch the binding to the quilt. Keep the raw edges even with the quilt-top edge. End the stitching ¼" from the corner of the quilt and backstitch. Clip the thread.

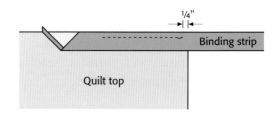

¼"

Binding strip

Quilt top

5. Turn the quilt so that you'll be stitching down the next side. Fold the binding up, away from the quilt, then back down onto itself, parallel with the edge of the quilt top. Begin stitching at the edge, backstitching to secure. Repeat on the remaining edges and corners of the quilt.

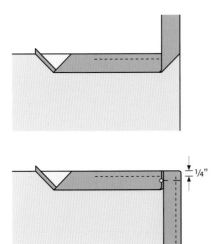

6. When you reach the beginning of the binding, overlap the beginning stitches by about 1" and cut away any excess binding, trimming the end at a 45° angle. Tuck the end of the binding into the fold and finish the seam.

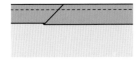

7. Fold the binding over the raw edges of the quilt to the back, with the folded edge covering the row of machine stitching, and blindstitch in place. A miter will form at each corner. Blindstitch the mitered corners.

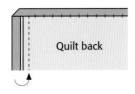 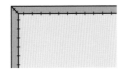

Bias-Grain Binding

BINDING USED on curved or scalloped edges must be cut on the bias grain of the fabric. Bias-grain binding has more stretch than straight-grain binding, allowing it to be eased around curved edges without puckering. To cut bias-grain binding strips:

1. Fold a square of fabric on the diagonal.

Or, fold a half-yard piece of fabric as shown in the diagrams below, paying careful attention to the location of the lettered corners.

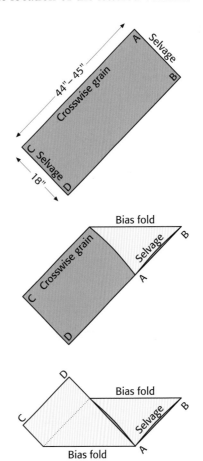

2. Cut strips 2½" wide, cutting perpendicular to the folds as shown.

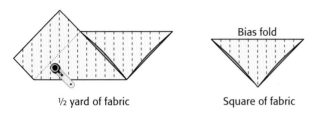

½ yard of fabric   Square of fabric

To attach the binding to the quilt edges, refer to "Straight-Grain Binding" on page 14. If you are making a quilt with scalloped edges, see "Optional Scalloped Border" on page 55.

Adding a Hanging Sleeve

IF YOU plan to display your finished quilt on the wall, add a hanging sleeve to accommodate the rod.

1. Using leftover fabric from the front or a piece of muslin, cut a strip 6" to 8" wide and 1" shorter than the width of the quilt at the top edge. Fold the ends under ½", then ½" again; stitch.

2. Fold the fabric strip in half lengthwise, wrong sides together, and baste the raw edges to the top edge of the quilt back. The top edge of the sleeve will be secured when the binding is sewn on the quilt.

Baste sleeve to top edge of quilt.

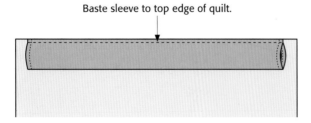

3. Finish the sleeve, after the binding has been attached, by blindstitching the bottom of the sleeve in place. Push the bottom edge of the sleeve up just a bit to provide a little give so the hanging rod does not put strain on the quilt itself.

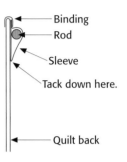

Binding
Rod
Sleeve
Tack down here.

Quilt back

Signing Your Quilt

FUTURE GENERATIONS will want to know more than just who made your quilt and when. Labels can be as elaborate or as simple as you desire. You can write, type, or embroider the information. Be sure to include your name, the name of the quilt, your city and state, the date, the name of the recipient if it is a gift, and any other interesting or important information about the quilt.

Embroidery Stitches

SOME OF THE PROJECTS in this book have been accented with embroidery. Choose from the embroidery stitches illustrated below to add details to the projects. Use two or three strands of embroidery floss.

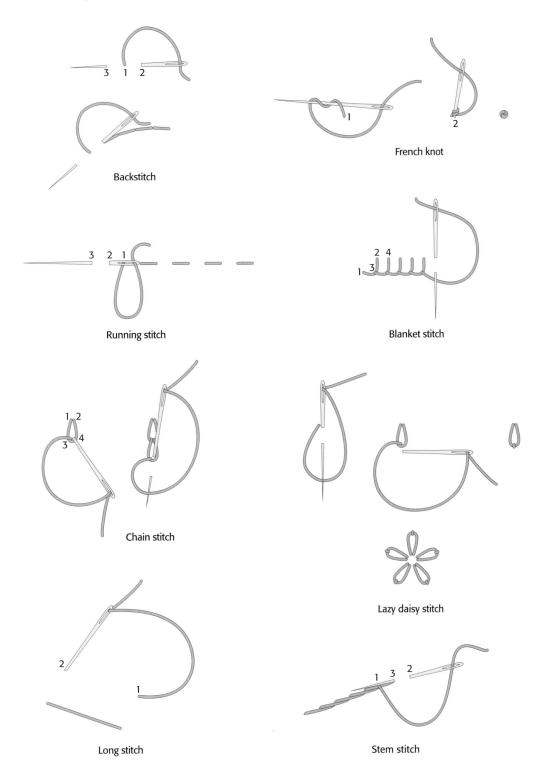

Backstitch

French knot

Running stitch

Blanket stitch

Chain stitch

Lazy daisy stitch

Long stitch

Stem stitch

Little Sweethearts

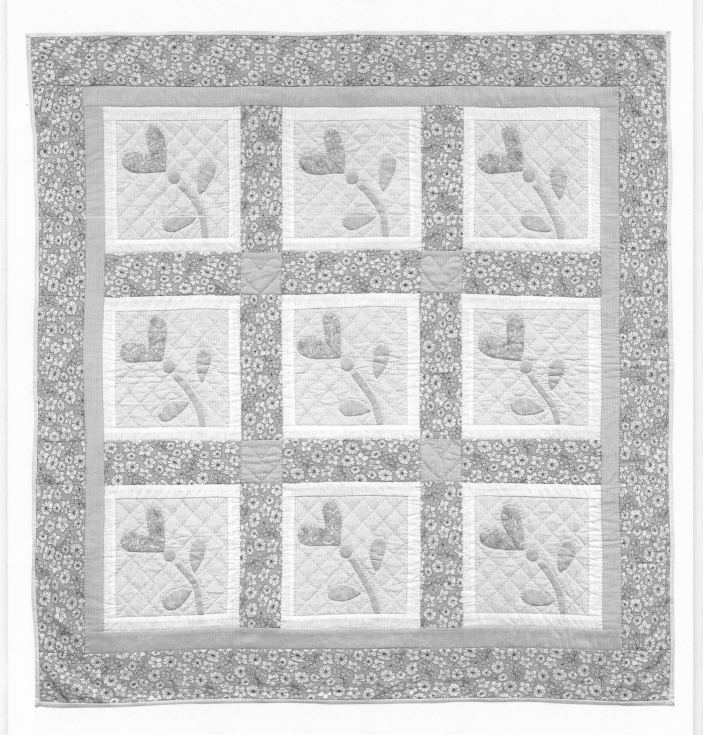

Pink heart "tulips" dance across yellow backgrounds in this cheerful quilt.
A white border frames each block for emphasis.

♥

By Chris Mewhinney, 2000, Fairfield, Washington. Finished quilt size: 47" x 47"; finished block size: 8" x 8".

Materials

42"-wide fabric

- ¼ yd. pink print #1 for flower petals
- ¼ yd. solid pink for flower circles, sashing squares, and inner border
- ½ yd. green for stems and leaves
- 1 yd. yellow for block backgrounds
- ½ yd. white for block borders
- 1 yd. pink print #2 for sashing and outer border
- 3 yds. for backing
- ⅜ yd. for binding
- 51" x 51" piece of batting
- 4" x 4" piece of tagboard

Cutting

Note: *All measurements include ¼"-wide seam allowances, unless otherwise indicated.*

From the yellow, cut:
- 9 squares, each 8½" x 8½", for the block backgrounds

From the white, cut:
- 8 strips, each 1½" x 42", for the block borders; crosscut the strips into 18 strips, each 1½" x 8½", and 18 strips, each 1½" x 10½"

From pink print #2, cut:
- 12 strips, each 3½" x 10½", for the sashing
- 5 strips, each 4½" x 42", for the outer border

From the solid pink, cut:
- 4 squares, each 3½" x 3½", for the sashing squares
- 4 strips, each 1⅞" x 42", for the inner border

From the binding fabric, cut:
- 5 strips, each 2" x 42"

Appliquéing the Blocks

1. Referring to "Basic Appliqué" on pages 8–9 and using the patterns on page 21, cut 18 flower petals (9 reverse), 9 flower circles, 9 stems, and 18 leaves; add ⅛" around all edges (rather than a scant ¼"). Using the flower-circle pattern, cut 9 flower circles from the tagboard; set aside.

2. Sew a small running stitch around a fabric flower circle, close to the raw edge. Place a tagboard circle in the center of the fabric circle on the wrong side of the fabric. Pull the thread ends to gather the fabric around the circle; tie a knot if needed to secure.

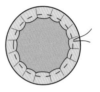

   Steam press the circle; allow to cool. Remove the tagboard. Repeat for the remaining flower circles.

3. Machine stitch 2 flower-petal pieces (1 reverse), right sides together, along the center seam, ⅛" from the raw edges, beginning and ending stitching ⅛" from the inner and outer points. Finger-press seam allowances to one side. Repeat for the remaining flower petals.

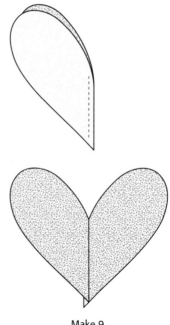

Make 9.

4. Referring to "Needle-Turn Appliqué" on page 8 and using the placement diagram on page 21 and the photograph on page 18 as guides, appliqué the flower petals, flower circles, stems, and leaves to the yellow background squares.

Assembly and Finishing

1. Join the 1½" x 8½" white strips to the side edges of the blocks. Join the 1½" x 10½" white strips to the top and bottom edges of the blocks.

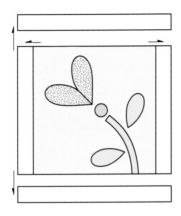

2. Join 3 blocks and two 3½" x 10½" pink print #2 sashing strips together to make each of 3 rows.

Make 3.

3. Join three 3½" x 10½" pink print #2 sashing strips and two 3½" solid pink squares to make each of 2 rows of horizontal sashing.

Make 2.

4. Join the rows, adding the horizontal sashing strips between them. Press the seams toward the sashing.

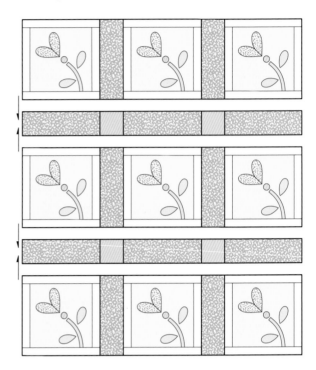

5. Referring to "Straight-Cut Borders" on page 10, measure, trim, and sew the inner border strips to the side edges of the quilt top, then do the same for the top and bottom edges. Repeat for the outer border strips.

6. Layer the quilt with batting and backing; baste. Quilt as desired.

7. Bind the edges and add a label.

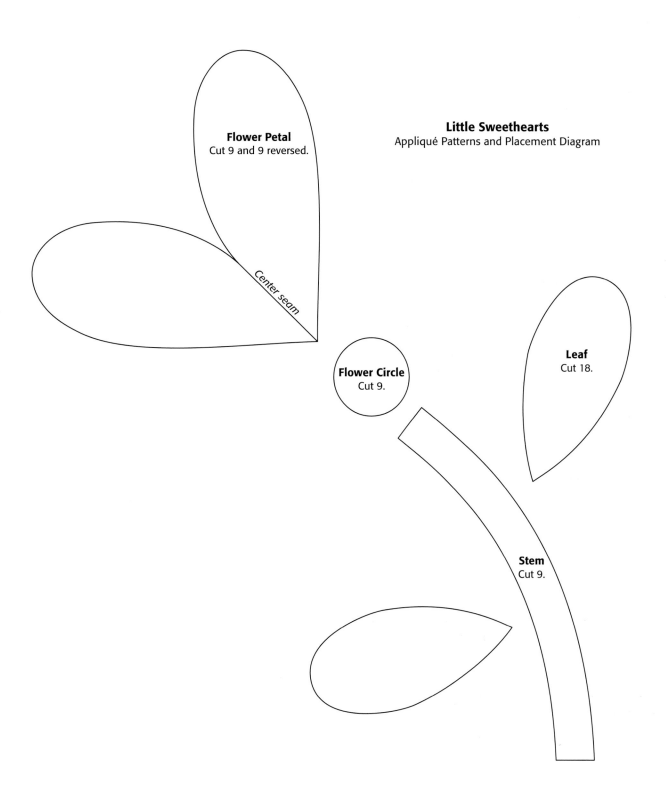

Flower Petal
Cut 9 and 9 reversed.

Center seam

Little Sweethearts
Appliqué Patterns and Placement Diagram

Flower Circle
Cut 9.

Leaf
Cut 18.

Stem
Cut 9.

Hip Cats

Foundation-pieced whimsical cats are combined with checkered hearts in this brightly colored quilt.
The pattern, "My Funny Valentine," comes from *It's Raining Cats and Dogs* by Janet Kime (Martingale & Company, 1998).

♥

By Jolene Otter and Karen Otter, 2001, Edmonds, Washington. Finished quilt size: 34¼" x 34¼"; finished block size: 5" x 5".

Materials

42"-wide fabric

- 1¼ yds. *total* assorted scraps for Heart blocks (fabrics A and B), Cat blocks, and corner squares
- 1 yd. green for block backgrounds, side and corner setting triangles, and corner squares
- ¾ yd. print for border and binding
- 1¼ yds. for backing
- 39" x 39" piece of batting
- Black embroidery floss

Cutting

NOTE: *Cut the Heart-block pieces and the side and corner setting triangles first; then use the remaining fabric to foundation-piece the Cat blocks. All measurements include ¼"-wide seam allowances, unless otherwise indicated.*

From fabric A, cut:
- 16 strips, each 1½" x 22", for Heart blocks

From fabric B, cut:
- 16 strips, each 1½" x 22", for Heart blocks

From the green, cut:
- 3 strips, each 1½" x 42"; crosscut the strips into 64 squares, each 1½" x 1½", for Heart blocks
- 1 strip, 2½" x 42"; crosscut the strip into 16 squares, each 2½" x 2½", for Heart blocks
- 3 squares, each 8½" x 8½"; cut each square twice diagonally, for a total of 12 side setting triangles
- 2 squares, each 4½" x 4½"; cut each square once diagonally, for a total of 4 corner setting triangles

From the print, cut:
- 4 strips, each 3¼" x 42", for border
- 4 strips, each 1¾" x 42", for binding

Block Assembly

Heart Blocks

NOTE: *Each Heart block is made from 1 strip of fabric A and 1 strip of fabric B, each strip measuring 1½" x 22". Select fabrics that contrast well with the background. Make 16 Heart blocks.*

1. Sew a strip A to a strip B to make an A-B unit. Crosscut the A-B unit into 3 pieces, each 7" wide.

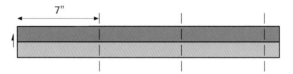

2. Sew the 3 crosscut pieces together to make 1 segment, alternating the colors. Press the seam allowances toward the darker fabric.

3. Even up one edge of the segment with a cleanup cut, then make 4 crosscut pieces, each 1½" wide. Make sure the crosscuts are perpendicular to the seam lines, or the little squares will not be square.

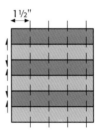

4. Lay out the 4 crosscut pieces with the dark fabric at the top and the light fabric at the bottom, as shown.

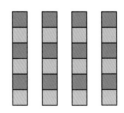

5. Modify the crosscut pieces as shown. From the first 3, rip out a seam and remove an end square. Discard these squares. Rip out the center seam in the fourth crosscut piece and save both halves. Press all the pieces.

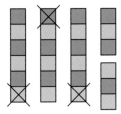

6. With a ruler, draw a faint diagonal line on the wrong side of each of the sixty-four 1½" background squares.

7. Sew a 1½" background square to the first crosscut piece as shown. Trim away the corner.

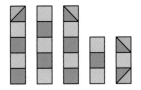

Stitch.   Trim.   Press.

8. Sew 1½" background squares to the top of the third crosscut piece and to the top and bottom of the fourth crosscut piece with dark squares at the top and bottom. Rotate the background squares for some of the pieces to produce the diagonal seams shown below.

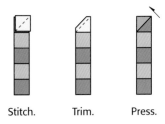

9. Sew the first 3 crosscut pieces together. Sew the 2 halves of the fourth crosscut piece together. Press the seam allowances away from the pieced corners. Sew the fourth crosscut segment to a 2½" background square. Press the seam allowances toward the background square.

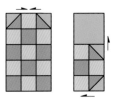

10. Sew the 2 segments together to make the Heart block.

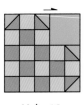

Make 16.

Cat Blocks

THE CAT blocks in this quilt are foundation pieced. In paper-foundation piecing, fabric pieces are added, one by one, to a design drawn or printed on a paper foundation. All seams are sewn directly on the marked lines, through the foundation. When you sew the designs on foundation paper, the lines and points

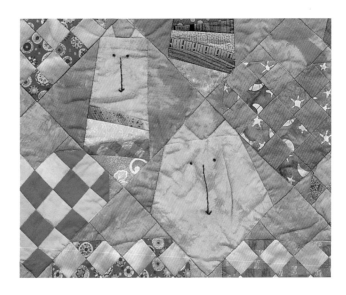

of the design are always neat and clean. Note that the block you sew will always be the mirror image of the design on the foundation pattern.

1. Using the 3 cat patterns on pages 28–30, trace or photocopy 9 foundations, reversing some of them. Copy the numbers as well; they tell you the order in which the fabric pieces are added. Shade lightly (or mark with an *X*) the dark areas of the design to indicate which fabric is used in each section. Cut out the foundations, cutting a bit larger than the drawn design plus the ¼" seam allowances.

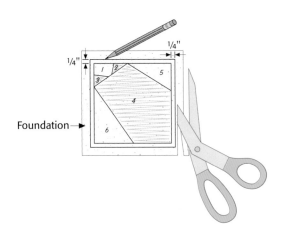

2. Cut a piece of fabric roughly the shape of piece 1 in the foundation, adding about ¼" all around for seam allowances. Place the fabric piece, right side up, on the wrong (unmarked) side of the foundation.

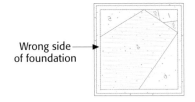 

Wrong side of foundation

3. Cut a piece of fabric roughly the shape of piece 2 plus seam allowances. Pin it to fabric piece 1, right sides together. Check that both pieces overlap the seam line by at least ¼".

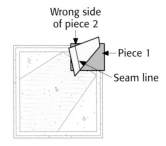

Wrong side of piece 2

Piece 1

Seam line

4. Turn the unit over so the printed side of the foundation is up and the fabric is on the underside. Sew the seam exactly on the drawn line, extending the seam at least ⅛" beyond the drawn line on both ends. Do not backstitch at either end.

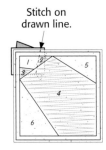

Stitch on drawn line.

5. Turn the unit over so the fabric is on top. Trim the seam allowances to ¼" or less. Flip piece 2, and press with a dry iron.

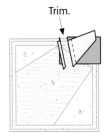 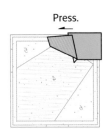

Trim.

Press.

6. Pin piece 3 in place, right side down, on the wrong side of the foundation, turn the unit over, and sew the seam on the drawn line. Turn the unit over, trim the seam allowances, flip piece 3, and press.

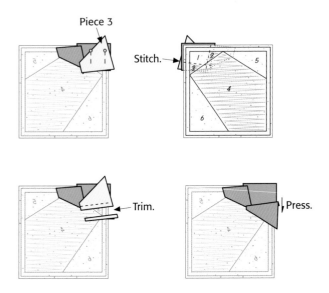

7. Add the remaining pieces in order.

Tip

The cats can be individualized by strip piecing the bodies to make them striped. In place of piece 4, alternate assorted scraps of cat fabric; cutting the strips in random widths and sewing them on at varying angles.

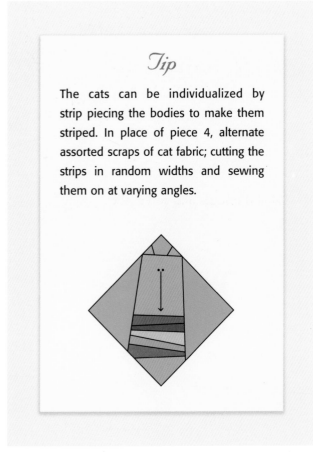

8. When the block is done, trim the edges, leaving ¼"-wide seam allowances. Use the outer dashed lines on the foundation pattern as a guide, but use a ruler to cut the block to the exact size needed, including ¼"-wide seam allowances. For the moment, leave the foundation paper in place.

Tips for Foundation Piecing

♦ Always press with a dry iron. Steam makes the paper foundation curl and can distort it.

♦ Use a smaller stitch length than usual. The more holes you make in the paper foundation, the easier it will be to tear it away.

♦ Grade the seam allowances as you trim them to reduce bulk: trim one layer first, then trim the other so it is wider or narrower. If one fabric is darker than the other, make the darker seam allowance the narrower one. It will then be less likely to show through on the surface of the quilt.

9. Transfer the lines for the cat faces to the blocks; then embroider them using a backstitch for the nose and mouth and French knots for the eyes (see "Embroidery Stitches" on page 17). Notice in the color photograph (page 22) that some of the faces are not straight up and down, but are tilted to one side or the other. This little touch makes the quilt delightfully whimsical; the cats look like they are peering around corners.

Assembly and Finishing

1. Arrange the Heart and Cat blocks into diagonal rows as shown. Add side and corner setting triangles to the rows as shown.

2. Sew the blocks together in diagonal rows. (The side setting triangles are slightly larger than needed and will be trimmed in step 5.) Press the seam allowances of each row in one direction. Press seam allowances from row to row in opposite directions.

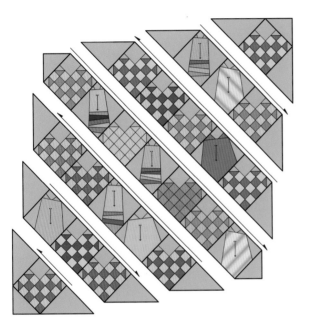

3. Staystitch around each row, ⅛" from the outer edges. Remove the foundation paper.

4. Sew the rows together. Press the seam allowances in either direction.

5. Trim the outer edges of the quilt, leaving ¼"-wide seam allowances all around.

6. Using the corner-square foundation pattern on page 30, foundation piece 4 corner squares.

7. Referring to "Borders with Corner Squares" on page 11, measure, trim, and sew the border strips to the side edges of the quilt top first, then to the top and bottom edges.

8. Layer the quilt top with batting and backing; baste. Quilt as desired.

9. Bind the edges and add a label.

Hip Cats
Foundation Pattern

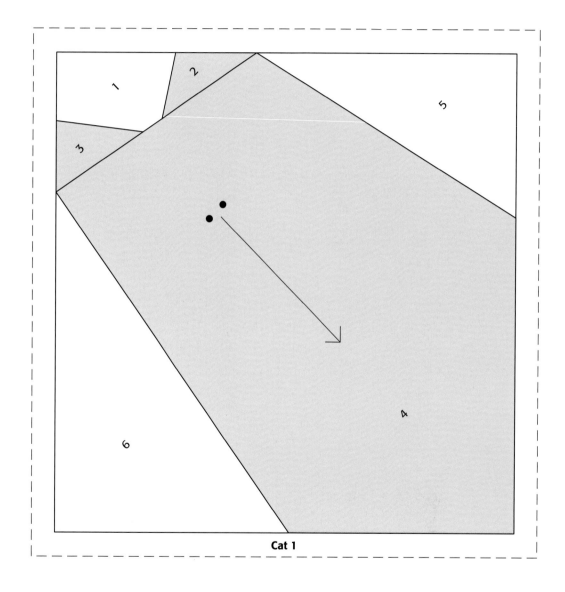

Cat 1

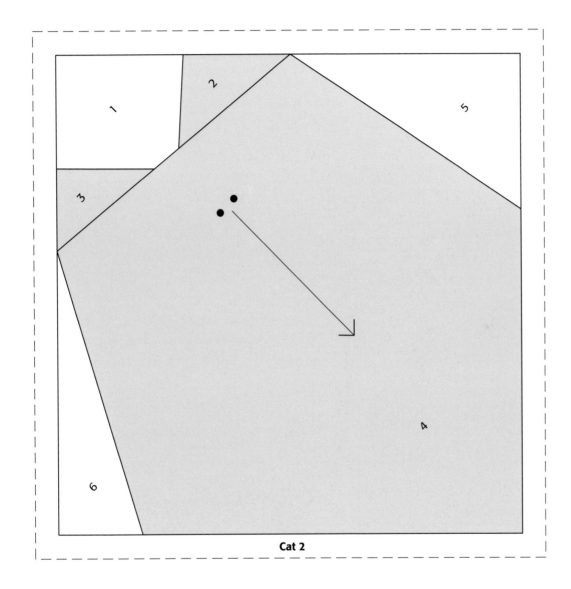

Cat 2

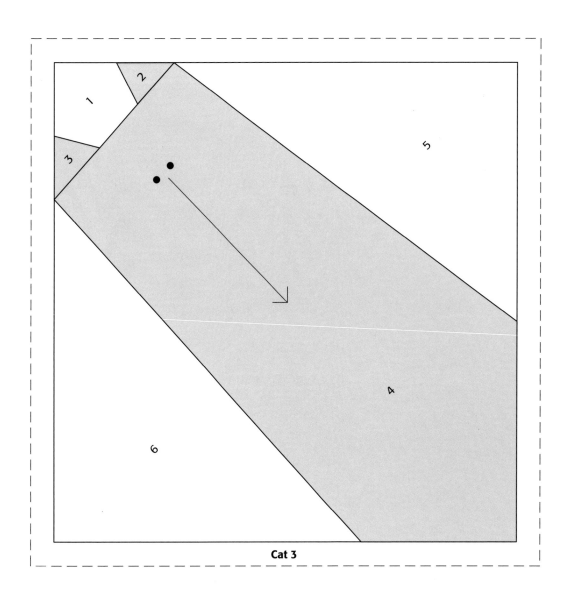

Cat 3

Hip Cats
Foundation Patterns

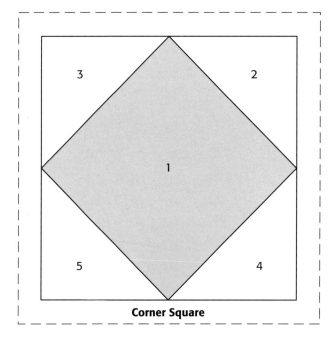

Corner Square

Quilts Bring Hearts Together

Four-patch hearts and embroidery accent this sweet wall hanging. A pieced border frames the quilt.
The pattern design, by Eileen Westfall, is from *Quilts Say It Best* (That Patchwork Place, 1997).

♥

By Bridget Haugh, 2001, Minneapolis, Minnesota. Finished quilt size: 24" x 27".

Materials

42"-wide fabric

- ¼ yd. dark blue for heart appliqués, Diamond blocks, and pieced border strips
- ⅛ yd. light blue for heart appliqués
- ¼ yd. rose for heart appliqués and border strips
- ¼ yd. medium pink for heart appliqués, Diamond blocks, and pieced border strips
- ⅝ yd. medium green for vines, Diamond blocks, and binding
- ½ yd. white for background
- ¼ yd. dark green for Pinwheel blocks
- ¼ yd. light pink for Pinwheel blocks
- 1 yd. for backing
- 28" x 31" piece of batting
- Medium green embroidery floss

Cutting

NOTE: *All measurements include ¼"-wide seam allowances, unless otherwise indicated.*

From the dark blue, cut:
- 8 squares, each 3½" x 3½", for heart appliqués
- 8 squares, each 2⅞" x 2⅞"; cut the squares once diagonally to yield 16 triangles for Diamond blocks
- 38 squares, each 1½" x 1½", for pieced border strips

From the light blue, cut:
- 8 squares, each 3½" x 3½", for heart appliqués

From the rose, cut:
- 8 squares, each 3½" x 3½", for heart appliqués
- 4 strips, each 1½" x 8½", for border strips
- 4 strips, each 1½" x 11½", for border strips

From the medium pink, cut:
- 8 squares, each 3½" x 3½", for heart appliqués
- 4 squares, each 2⅞" x 2⅞"; cut the squares once diagonally to yield 16 triangles for Diamond blocks

- 38 squares, each 1½" x 1½", for pieced border strips

From the medium green, cut:
- 1 strip, 1" x 24", on the bias grain, for vines
- 4 squares, each 2⅞" x 2⅞"; cut the squares once diagonally to yield 8 triangles for Diamond blocks
- 3 strips, each 1¾" x 42", for binding

From the white, cut:
- 1 rectangle, 16½" x 19½", for background. NOTE: *Cut slightly larger than this; then trim to this size after completing appliqué and embroidery.*

From the dark green, cut:
- 16 squares, each 2⅞" x 2⅞"; cut the squares once diagonally to yield 32 triangles for Pinwheel blocks

From the light pink, cut:
- 16 squares, each 2⅞" x 2⅞"; cut the squares once diagonally to yield 32 triangles for Pinwheel blocks

Assembly and Finishing

1. Sew together 3½" squares to make four-patch units. Referring to "Making Templates" on page 8 and using the pattern on page 34, cut one heart from each four-patch unit.

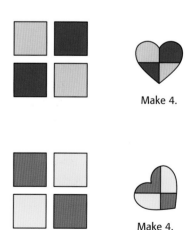

Make 4.

Make 4.

2. To make vines, fold the 1" x 24" medium green bias strip in half lengthwise, wrong sides together. Stitch the long raw edges together, using a scant ¼"-wide seam allowance. From the strip, cut 2 pieces, each 2" long; 2 pieces, each 2½" long; and 4 pieces, each 3½" long. Fold the pieces in half, concealing the seam allowances and stitching line on the back side. Pin the vines to the white background rectangle, using the placement guides below and on page 35 for positioning.

Scant ¼"

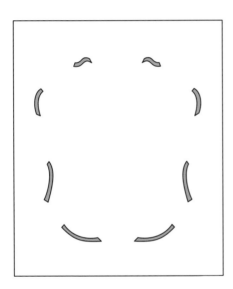

3. Pin the heart appliqués in place. Place a photocopy of the lettering guide on page 36 under the center of the fabric, and tape both to a sunlit window. Using a sharp #2 pencil or fine-lead mechanical pencil, trace the lettering onto the fabric. Adjust the placement of the vines and hearts as necessary; remove the hearts and trace the embroidery patterns for the leaves and tendrils. Referring to "Traditional Appliqué Stitch" on page 8, appliqué the vines in place.

4. Reposition the hearts on the quilt and, referring to "Needle-Turn Appliqué" on page 8, appliqué in place. On the background, embroider the leaves and tendrils, using a stem stitch, and the words, using a backstitch. (Refer to "Embroidery Stitches" on page 17.)

5. Sew the dark blue, medium pink, and medium green triangles together as shown to make the Diamond blocks.

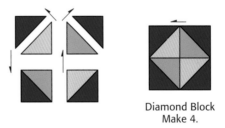

Diamond Block
Make 4.

6. Sew the dark green and light pink triangles together as shown to make the Pinwheel blocks.

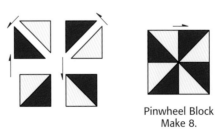

Pinwheel Block
Make 8.

7. Sew eleven 1½" medium pink and eleven 1½" dark blue squares together to make a pieced strip. Press seam allowances toward the dark blue squares. Sew a 1½" x 11½" rose strip to each side of the pieced strip. Press seam allowances toward the rose strips. Then add a Pinwheel block to each end to make a side border strip. Repeat to make a second side border strips.

8. Sew eight 1½" medium pink and eight 1½" dark blue squares together to make a pieced strip. Press seam allowances toward the dark blue squares. Sew a 1½" x 8½" rose strip to each side of the pieced strip. Press seam allowances toward the rose strips. Then add Pinwheel and Diamond blocks to the ends to make a top border strip. Repeat for the bottom border strip.

Side Border Strips
Make 2.

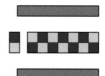

Top and Bottom Border Strips
Make 2.

9. Sew the side border strips to the quilt top; then add the top and bottom border strips.

10. Layer the quilt top with batting and backing; baste. Quilt as desired.

11. Bind the edges and add a label.

Quilts Bring Hearts Together
Appliqué Pattern

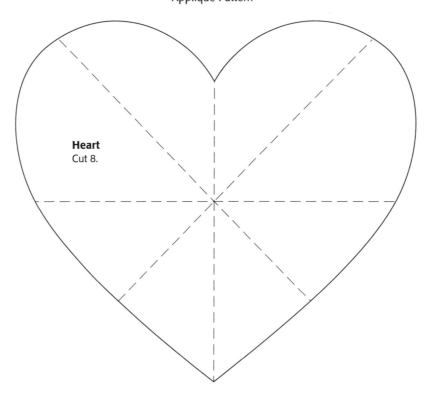

Heart
Cut 8.

Quilts Bring Hearts Together
Appliqué Placement Guide
and Embroidery Patterns

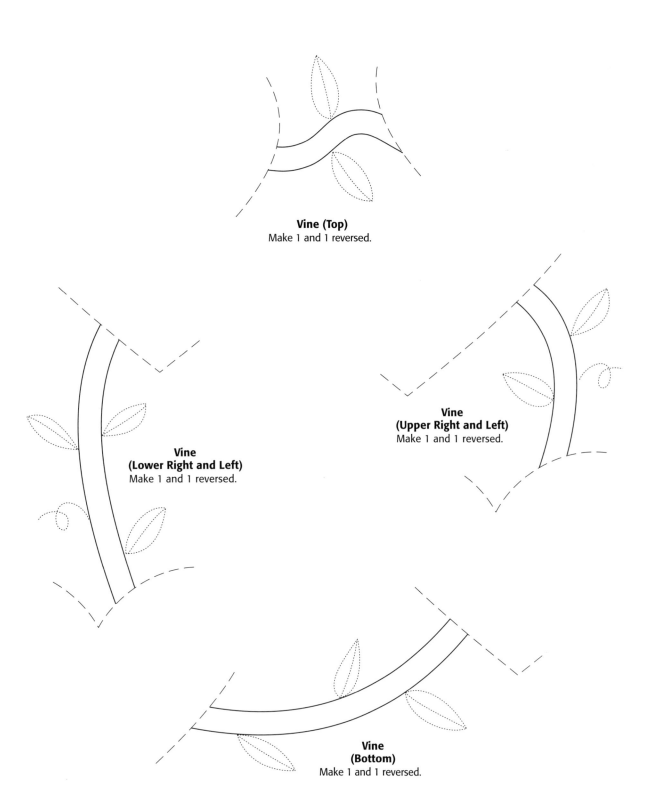

Vine (Top)
Make 1 and 1 reversed.

**Vine
(Upper Right and Left)**
Make 1 and 1 reversed.

**Vine
(Lower Right and Left)**
Make 1 and 1 reversed.

**Vine
(Bottom)**
Make 1 and 1 reversed.

QUILTS BRING HEARTS TOGETHER

Summer of the Hearts

Large and small Heart blocks, set on point, are framed with a triple border in this delightful wall hanging.
Another version of this design, created by Karen Walker and titled "Random Hearts," was first published in
A New Twist on Triangles (Martingale & Company, 1999) by Mary Sue Suit.

♥

By Karen Walker, 2001, Minatare, Nebraska. Finished quilt size: 62" x 62";
finished block sizes: large Heart, 9" x 9", small Heart, 6" x 6".

Materials

42"-wide fabric

- ⅜ yd. yellow for backgrounds of large Heart blocks and centers of small hearts
- ⅜ yd. light pink for centers of large hearts
- 2½ yds. pastel print for backgrounds of small Heart blocks, side and corner setting triangles, sashing strips, pieced middle border, and outer border
- ½ yd. *each* of 4 different deep pinks for large and small Heart blocks and pieced middle border
- 1½ yds. green for inner border, pieced middle border, and binding
- 3¾ yds. for backing
- 66" x 66" piece of batting

Cutting

NOTE: *All measurements include ¼"-wide seam allowances, unless otherwise indicated. For instructions on cutting wing triangle sets and kaleidoscope triangle sets, see pages 39–40. Use the wing and kaleidoscope patterns on page 47, or use Mary Sue's Triangle Ruler (see "Cutting the Basic Blocks," at right).*

From the yellow, cut:
- 6 strips, each 1½" x 42"; from the strips, cut 36 sets of 1½" wings for large Heart blocks
- 2 strips, each 1¼" x 42"; from the strips, cut 16 sets of 1¼" wings for centers of small hearts
- 1 strip, 3½" x 42"; from the strip, cut 9 squares, each 3½" x 3½", for large Heart blocks

From the light pink, cut:
- 6 strips, 1½" x 42"; from the strips, cut 36 sets of 1½" wings for centers of large hearts

From the pastel print, cut:
- 2 strips, each 1¼" x 42"; from the strips, cut 16 sets of 1¼" wings for small Heart blocks
- 4 squares, each 2½" x 2½", for small Heart blocks
- 4 strips, each 2" x 42"; from the strips, cut 16 strips, each 2" x 10½", for sashing strips in small Heart blocks

- 4 squares, each 9⅞" x 9⅞"; cut each square once diagonally to yield 8 side setting triangles
- 2 squares, each 7¼" x 7¼"; cut each square once diagonally to yield 4 corner setting triangles
- 1 strip, 1½" x 42"; cut the strip in half, and from the 2 strips cut 4 sets of 1½" wings for pieced middle border
- 4 strips, each 3" x 42"; from the strips, cut 28 sets of 4" kaleidoscopes for pieced middle border
- 4 strips, each 6½" x 64"; cut on the lengthwise grain, and cut strips slightly longer than 64", to be trimmed later for outer border

From the 4 different deep pinks, cut a *total* of:
- 14 strips, each 3" x 42"; place 2 different strips right sides together and cut 104 sets of 4" kaleidoscopes for large Heart blocks and pieced middle border
- 4 strips, each 2¼" x 42"; place 2 different strips right sides together and cut 32 sets of 3" kaleidoscopes for small Heart blocks

From the green, cut:
- 4 strips, each 3½" x 42", for inner border
- 8 strips, each 1½" x 42"; from the strips, cut 56 sets of 1½" wings for pieced middle border
- 4 squares, each 3½" x 3½", for pieced middle border
- 7 strips, each 2¼" x 42", for binding

Cutting the Basic Blocks

3" block   2" block

THE LARGE HEART blocks and the pieced middle border in this quilt are made from 3" (finished) basic blocks, and the small Heart blocks are made from 2" (finished) basic blocks. Each block consists of two kaleidoscopes and two wings. You can use the kaleidoscope and wing patterns on page 47 to make the basic blocks, or you might consider using Mary

Sue's Triangle Ruler, a tool specially designed for these blocks. Instructions are given for both cutting methods.

Mary Sue's Triangle Ruler is a quadrangle with 45°, 90°, and 112.5° corners. Two very important lines divide the ruler into sections: a center line runs from the 45° corner to the 90° corner, and a crossbar connects the two 112.5° angles. In addition, ¼" marks run parallel to both the center line and the crossbar.

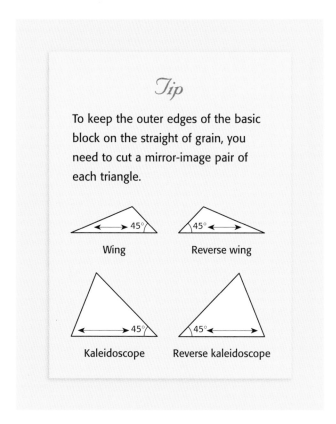

Tip

To keep the outer edges of the basic block on the straight of grain, you need to cut a mirror-image pair of each triangle.

Wing   Reverse wing

Kaleidoscope   Reverse kaleidoscope

Wing Triangle Sets

Template Method

1. Referring to "Making Templates" on page 8 and using the patterns on page 47, make 1¼" and 1½" wing templates. Place 2 strips of fabric same sides together, and place the appropriate-size template on the strips, aligning the long side of the template with the bottom edge of the strips and placing the point of the 45° angle just inside the selvage. Cut around the template.

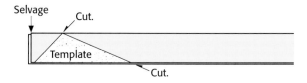

2. Without moving the fabric strips, rotate the template, aligning the longest edge with the top of the strip and the next-longest edge with the previous cut. Cut along the short edge. Continue rotating the template to cut additional wing sets in the same manner.

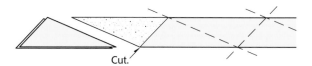

Mary Sue's Triangle Ruler Method

1. Place 2 strips of fabric same sides together. With the center line of the ruler horizontal and the 90° angle pointing left, place the ruler's 1¼" or 1½" mark (depending on the width of your strip) at the bottom edge of the fabric and just inside the selvage. Cut around the ruler.

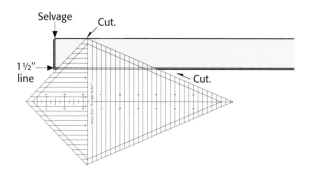

2. Without moving the fabric strips, rotate the ruler, aligning the ruler's 1¼" or 1½" mark (depending on the width of your strip) with the top of the strip, and the other long edge with the previous cut. Cut along the short edge. Continue rotating the ruler to cut additional wing sets in the same manner.

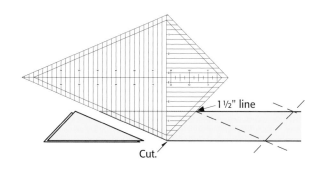

Kaleidoscope Triangle Sets

Template Method

1. Referring to "Making Templates" on page 8 and using the patterns on page 47, make 3" and 4" kaleidoscope templates. Place 2 fabric strips same sides together. Place the appropriate-sized template on the strips just inside the selvage, aligning one long side of the template with the upper edge of the strip (one long edge needs to be on the straight of grain). Cut around the template.

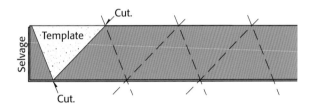

2. Without moving the fabric strips, rotate the template so that the long edge that was at the top for the last cut is at the bottom. Cut around the template. Continue rotating the template to cut additional kaleidoscope sets in the same manner.

Tip

If you have trouble recognizing the straight-grain edge of cut triangles, mark both long edges of the fabric strip with a soap sliver or piece of chalk before you cut.

Mary Sue's Triangle Ruler Method

1. Place 2 fabric strips same sides together. Place the 45°-angle tip at the top of the fabric strips and align the center line of the ruler with the selvage. Make sure the center line is perpendicular to the cut edge of the strips. Cut along the ruler to establish the correct angle.

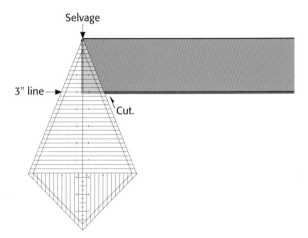

2. Align the crossbar with the previous cut as shown and place the 112.5° angle at the bottom edge of the fabric strips. Cut along the ruler.

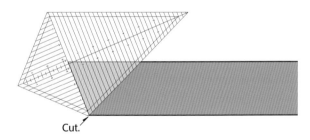

3. Align the crossbar with the previous cut and slide the ruler down so the 112.5° angle is at the top of the fabric strips. Cut along the ruler.

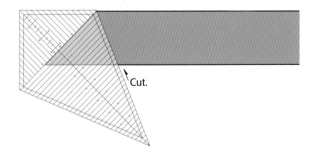

4. Continue across the strip to cut additional kaleidoscope sets in the same manner.

Basic Block Assembly

THE FOLLOWING STEPS give you techniques for constructing basic blocks. Refer to "Heart Block Assembly" on page 43 and "Adding Borders" on page 46 before sewing the basic blocks together.

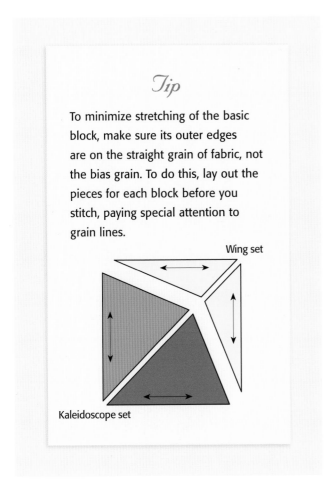

Tip

To minimize stretching of the basic block, make sure its outer edges are on the straight grain of fabric, not the bias grain. To do this, lay out the pieces for each block before you stitch, paying special attention to grain lines.

Wing set

Kaleidoscope set

1. With the wing on top, sew a right wing to a right kaleidoscope as shown. For the 3" finished block, use a 4" kaleidoscope and a 1½" wing. For the 2" finished block, use a 3" kaleidoscope and a 1¼" wing. Position the point of the kaleidoscope so

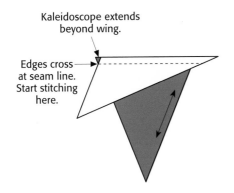

Kaleidoscope extends beyond wing.

Edges cross at seam line. Start stitching here.

that it extends beyond the wing (the excess fabric will be trimmed in a later step). Always sew from the 112.5° end of the wing toward the skinny end, and use a ¼" seam allowance. The first stitch should go through both fabrics. Press the seam allowances toward the wing.

2. Repeat for the left wing and left kaleidoscope, starting with the wing on the bottom and pressing toward the kaleidoscope.

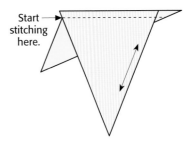

Start stitching here.

3. With right sides together, pin the pieced sections together along the long edges. The seam allowances should butt up against each other. Stitch. Press the seam allowances to one side. Throughout the project, always press this seam toward the same side.

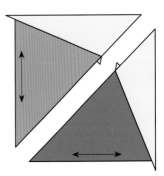

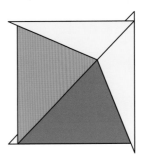

Trimming

IF YOU DIDN'T offset your pieces properly, trimming will fix the problem. You'll get perfect points every time.

1. Place the basic block on the cutting mat with the wing corner at the lower left.

2. Lay a square ruler on the block with 0 at the upper right. Align the ruler's diagonal line with the block's center seam. For the 3" basic block, place the 3⅜" marks at the wing seams; for the 2" basic block, place the 2⅜" marks at the wing seams. Trim any excess from the upper and right-hand edges of the block.

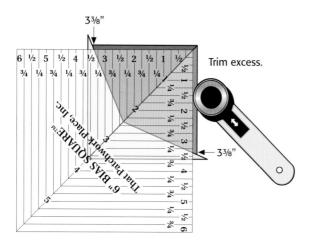

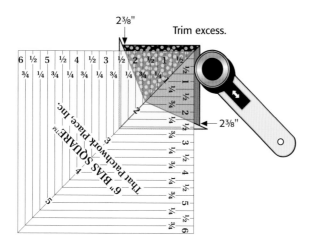

3. Rotate the block, placing the wing corner at the upper right.

4. Lay your square ruler on the block with 0 at the upper right. Align the ruler's diagonal line with the block's center seam. For the 3" basic block, align the 3½" marks with the bottom and left-hand edges of the block; for the 2" basic block, align the 2½" marks with the bottom and left-hand edges of the block. Trim any excess from the upper and right-hand edges.

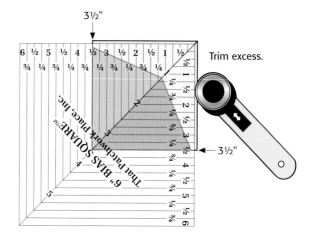

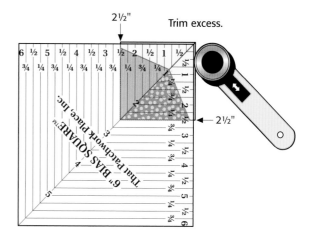

5. Press, twisting the seams open at each corner (see "Twist Press" on page 43).

Twist Press

To reduce bulk at the seams where points come together, try Mary Sue Suit's "twist press." First, press the seam allowances to one side, then open just the end, where the seam will meet others, and press open. This creates a little fold or twist in the seam allowance. By opening the seam allowance at bulky intersections, your piecing will be more accurate.

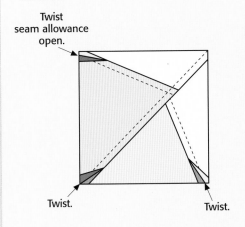

Twist seam allowance open.

Twist. Twist.

Heart Block Assembly

1. Referring to "Basic Block Assembly" on page 41, make the 3" finished blocks shown below for the large Heart blocks. Trim each block to 3½" x 3½", with the wing seam at 3⅜" (see "Trimming" on page 42).

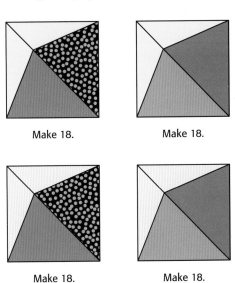

Make 18. Make 18.

Make 18. Make 18.

2. Using the basic blocks and 3½" yellow squares, lay out the pieces for 9 large Heart blocks as shown. Sew the pieces into rows. Press. Join the rows. Press, twisting open the ends of the seams.

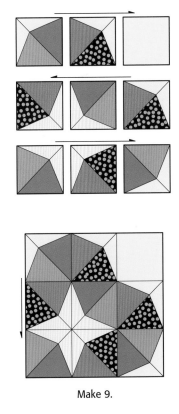

Make 9.

3. Find the midpoint of each block edge and pin.

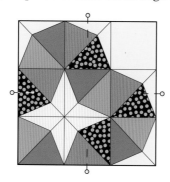

4. Referring to "Basic Block Assembly" on page 41, make the 2" finished blocks shown below for the small Heart blocks. Trim each block to 2½" x 2½", with the wing seam at 2⅜" (see "Trimming" on page 42).

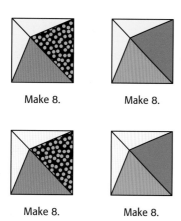

Make 8.   Make 8.

Make 8.   Make 8.

5. Using the basic blocks and 2½" pastel print squares, lay out the pieces for 4 small Heart blocks as shown. Sew the pieces into rows. Press. Join the rows. Press, twisting open the ends of the seams.

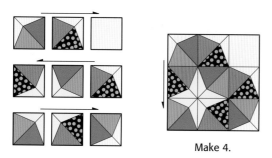

Make 4.

Quilt Assembly

1. Stack four 2" x 10½" pastel print sashing strips. Cut the left-hand edge at a 45° angle. Measure 6¼" from the left-hand edge along the bottom; mark and cut a 45° angle. Repeat for 3 additional sets of 4 sashing strips.

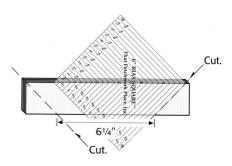

Cut.

6¼"

Cut.

2. With right sides together, lay the sashing strip on a small Heart block as shown. The block should extend beyond the sashing strip at the miter cuts.

3. Using a ¼" seam allowance, sew the pieces together, beginning and ending ¼" from the edge of the pieced unit. Do not press. Repeat on the remaining 3 sides of the block.

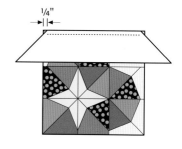

¼"

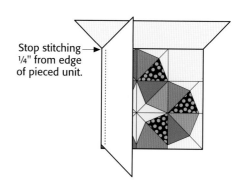

Stop stitching ¼" from edge of pieced unit.

4. With right sides together, fold the block in half diagonally. Align the raw edges of the sashing strips. Sew the miter from the inside corner to the outside edge. Repeat for the remaining 3 corners.

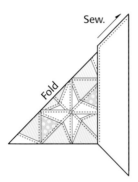

5. Press seam allowances from step 3 toward the sashing strips. Allow the diagonal miter seam to lie in whatever direction it chooses. Find the midpoint of each block edge and pin as for the large Heart blocks on page 44, step 3.

6. Pin-mark the midpoints of the long edges of the corner setting triangles. Pin-mark the midpoints of the short edges of the side setting triangles.

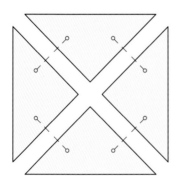

7. Arrange and sew the blocks in diagonal rows, being careful to match midpoints and seams. Press the seams in opposite directions from row to row. Trim the long sides of each row, cutting off any excess setting fabric.

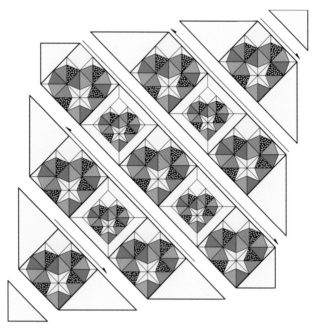

8. Join the rows; then add the remaining corner setting triangles. Press. Trim the outside edges of the quilt top ¼" from the points of the Heart blocks as necessary.

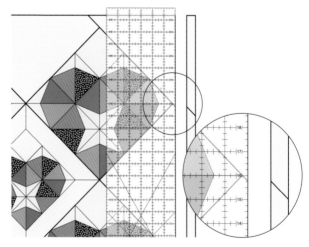

Align ¼" mark on ruler
with block point. Trim.

Adding Borders

Inner Border

REFERRING TO "Borders with Mitered Corners" on page 11, measure the quilt top for mitered border strips. Sew the green inner border strips to the quilt, mitering the corners. Press the seam allowances toward the inner border.

Pieced Middle Border

1. Referring to "Basic Block Assembly" on page 41, make the 3" finished blocks shown below. Trim each block to 3½" x 3½", with the wing seam at 3⅜" (see "Trimming" on page 42).

3. Sew the left and right pieced middle border strips to the quilt top, easing as necessary. Press the seam allowances toward the pieced middle border strips. Repeat to add the top and bottom pieced middle border strips.

Outer Border

Referring to "Borders with Mitered Corners" on page 11, measure the quilt top for mitered border strips. Sew the 6½" outer border strips to the quilt, mitering the corners. Press the seam allowances toward the outer border.

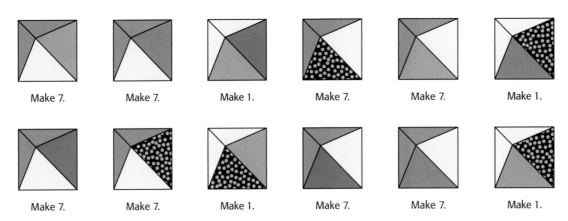

Make 7.   Make 7.   Make 1.   Make 7.   Make 7.   Make 1.

Make 7.   Make 7.   Make 1.   Make 7.   Make 7.   Make 1.

2. Join the basic blocks for the pieced middle border and the 3½" green squares into border strips as shown.

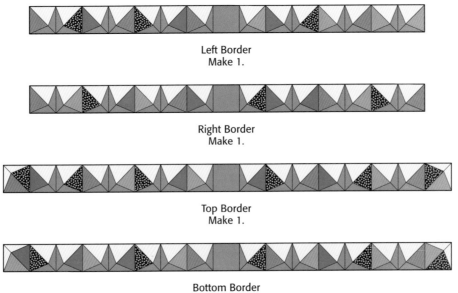

Left Border
Make 1.

Right Border
Make 1.

Top Border
Make 1.

Bottom Border
Make 1.

Finishing

1. Layer the quilt top with batting and backing; baste. Quilt as desired.

2. Bind the edges and add a label.

Summer of the Hearts
Basic Block Patterns

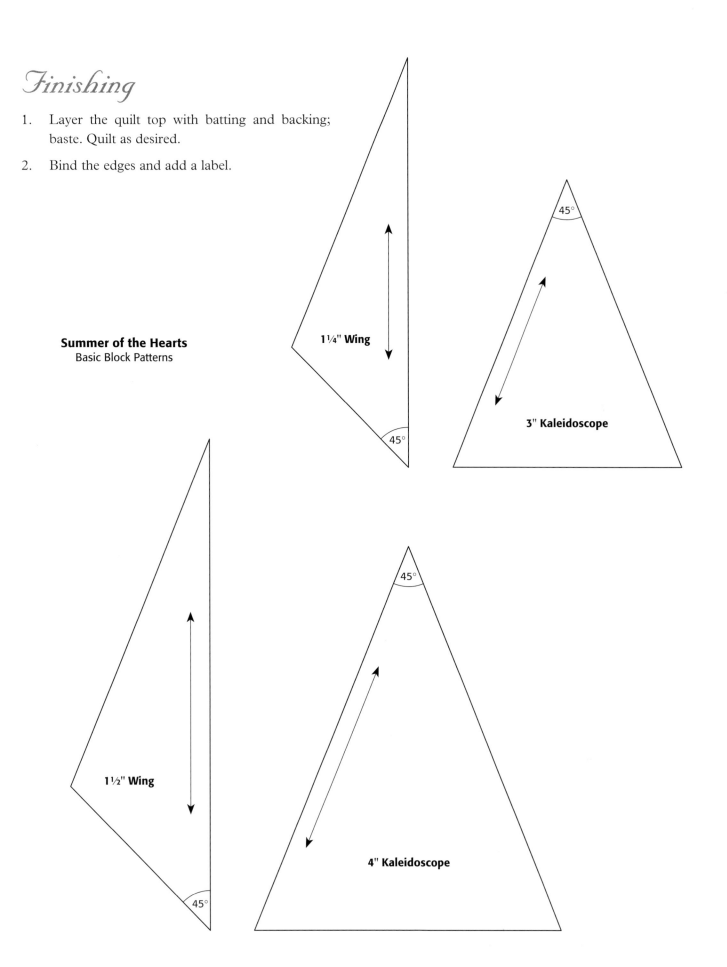

1¼" Wing

45°

45°

3" Kaleidoscope

1½" Wing

45°

45°

4" Kaleidoscope

Thirties Hearts and Arrows

Thirties reproduction prints make up this quilt with appliquéd hearts. The pattern, "Cross My Heart,"
is from *Calendar Quilts* by Joan Hanson (That Patchwork Place, 1991).

♥

By Joan Hanson, 2001, Seattle, Washington. Finished quilt size: 36" x 48"; finished block size: 6" x 6".

Materials

42"-wide fabric

- 1¼ yds. white for background and inner border
- ¼ yd. *each* of 12 fabrics for arrows (or use scraps)
- ¼ yd. *total* assorted pinks for appliqué hearts
- ½ yd. pink for outer border
- 1½ yds. for backing
- ½ yd. for binding
- 40" x 52" piece of batting

Cutting

NOTE: *All measurements include ¼"-wide seam allowances, unless otherwise indicated. Some pieces may be cut either by template alone or by "speed cutting" squares, which are cut in half diagonally and then trimmed with the template.*

From the white, cut:
- 2 strips, each 3" x 37", on the lengthwise grain for the inner border
- 2 strips, each 3" x 31", on the lengthwise grain for the inner border
- 24 squares, each 5½" x 5½", for the background. Cut each square once diagonally to yield 48 triangles, then use a template made from pattern A (page 50) to trim the corners. *Or,* cut 48 of template A.

From each of the 12 fabrics for arrows, cut:
- 2 rectangles, each 2½" x 4¾". *Or,* cut 2 of template B (page 51).
- 2 squares, each 3⅞" x 3⅞". Cut each square once diagonally to yield 2 triangles, then use a template made from pattern C (page 50) to trim the corners. *Or,* cut 4 of template C.

From the pink outer border fabric, cut:
- 4 strips, each 4" x 42"

From the binding fabric, cut:
- 4 strips, each 2½" x 42"

Block Assembly

JOIN BACKGROUND PIECES to both long sides of the rectangle of arrow fabric as shown. Join triangles from the same fabric as the rectangle to each end.

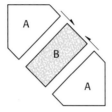
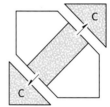

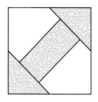

Make 24.

Assembly and Finishing

1. Arrange the blocks into 6 rows of 4 blocks each as shown. Sew the blocks together in horizontal rows.

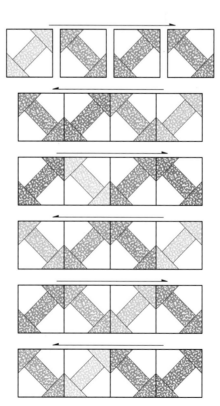

2. Join the rows together. Press seams all in the same direction.

3. Referring to "Basic Appliqué" on page 8 and using a template made from pattern D on page 51, prepare 8 heart appliqués and pin them to the background areas where 4 Arrow blocks intersect. Secure in place, following the instructions for "Needle-Turn Appliqué" (page 8).

4. Referring to "Straight-Cut Borders" on page 10, measure, trim, and sew the inner border strips to the side edges of the quilt top, then to the top and bottom edges. Repeat for the outer border strips.

5. Layer the quilt top with batting and backing; baste. Quilt as desired.

6. Bind the edges and add a label.

Thirties Hearts and Arrows
Patterns

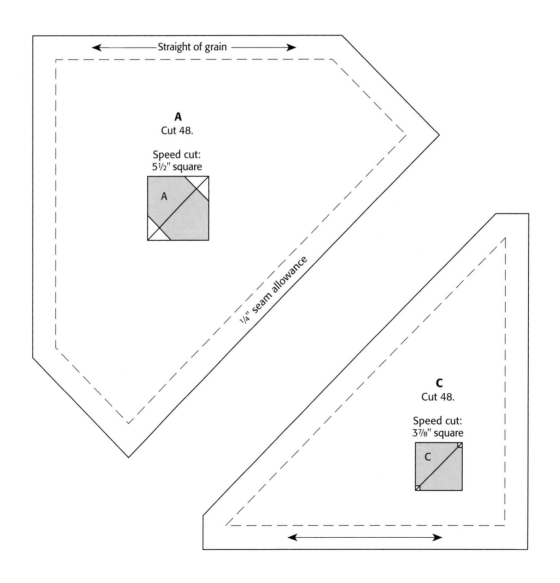

Thirties Hearts and Arrows
Patterns

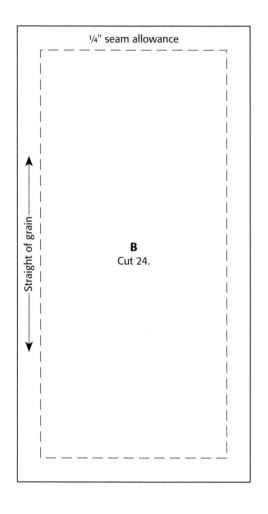

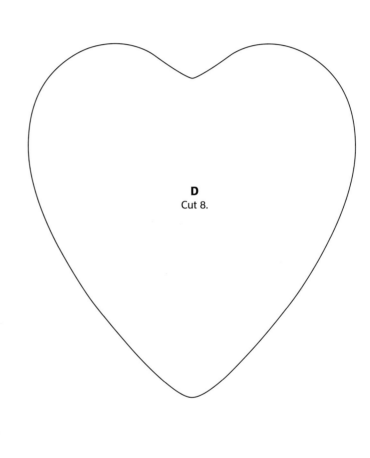

Summer Hearts

Four-patch Heart blocks are set on point and surrounded by Fan blocks. A scalloped border enhances this quilt
made from 1930s reproduction prints. The original design, by Chris Mewhinney, is from the book
The Quilting Bee, by Jackie Wolff and Lori Aluna (That Patchwork Place, 1994).

♥

By Beth Merrill Kovich, 2001, Woodinville, Washington. Quilted by Chris Mewhinney. Finished quilt size: 63" x 63";
finished block sizes: Heart blocks, 8" x 8", Fan blocks, 8" x 8".

Materials

42"-wide fabric

- ◆ 12 fat quarters of assorted prints for hearts
- ◆ 1 yd. green gingham for inner background
- ◆ 1¾ yds. white-and-green print for outer background
- ◆ 9 fat quarters of assorted prints for fans
- ◆ 1 fat quarter of yellow print for fan corners
- ◆ 2 yds. blue floral for side and corner setting triangles and border
- ◆ ⅞ yd. pink print for bias-grain binding
- ◆ 4 yds. for backing
- ◆ 69" x 69" piece of batting

Cutting

NOTE: *All measurements include ¼"-wide seam allowances, unless otherwise indicated.*

From the 12 fat quarters of assorted prints for hearts, cut:
- ◆ 100 squares, each 4¾" x 4¾"

From the green gingham, cut:
- ◆ 13 squares, each 8½" x 8½", for inner background

From the white-and-green print, cut:
- ◆ 28 squares, each 8½" x 8½", for outer background

From the blue floral, cut:
- ◆ 4 squares, each 13½" x 13½"; cut each square twice diagonally to yield 16 side setting triangles
- ◆ 2 squares, each 6⅝" x 6⅝"; cut squares once diagonally to yield 4 corner setting triangles
- ◆ 8 strips, each 5" x 42", for border

Heart Block Assembly

1. Join four 4¾" squares to make a four-patch unit.

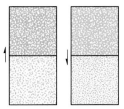

Make 25.

2. Referring to "Making Templates" on page 8 and using the pattern on page 57, make a heart template, including a ¼" seam allowance as indicated on pattern. Position the template on one half of the four-patch unit, aligning the placement line on the template with the horizontal seam and aligning the straight edge of the pattern with the vertical seam. Trace around the curved edge of the pattern; flip the pattern and trace the remaining half of the heart. Cut on the marked line.

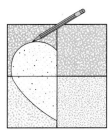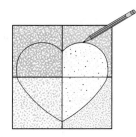

3. Taking 13 green gingham background squares and 12 white-and-green background squares, fold each in half on the diagonal and press. Unfold the squares and turn them on point so the crease is vertical. Center a heart on each background square, using the crease lines as guides and allowing ½" all around each heart.

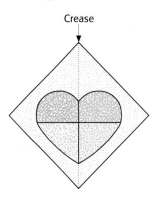

4. Referring to "Needle-Turn Appliqué" on page 8, steps 3 and 4, appliqué the hearts in place.

Fan Blocks Assembly

1. Referring to "Making Templates" on page 8 and the pattern on page 57, make a fan-blade template, including a ¼" seam allowance as indicated on pattern. Using the template, cut 128 fan blades from the 9 assorted prints for fans. Fold each fan blade in half lengthwise, right sides together, and sew a ¼" seam along the top edge.

2. Trim the seam allowance to ⅛". Unfold the fan blade, creating a stitched point. Press seam allowance open. Turn right side out, centering seam on wrong side of fan blade. Press.

3. Sew 8 blades together to make a fan, beginning at the bottoms of the blades and stopping ⅛" from the tops of the blades; backstitch.

4. Press seams to one side, being careful not to stretch blades. Pin or baste the fan unit in place on a remaining white-and-green background square. Referring to "Traditional Appliqué Stitch" on page 8, appliqué the points of the fan in place (the sides of the fan will be secured when the blocks are joined).

5. Referring to "Making Templates" on page 8 and using the pattern on page 57, make a fan-corner template, including a ¼" seam allowance as indicated on pattern. Using the template, cut 16 fan-corner pieces from the yellow print. Turn ¼" of the curved edge of the piece to the back and baste. Appliqué the fan-corner piece to the bottom corner of the fan.

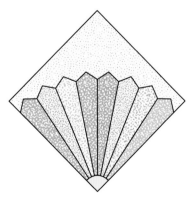

Make 16.

Assembly and Finishing

1. Arrange the appliquéd blocks, side setting triangles, and corner setting triangles as shown. The quilt shown in the color photograph on page 52 has one block in the lower right corner turned. To make your quilt symmetrical, arrange the blocks as shown in the illustration below. Sew the blocks together in diagonal rows. Press the seams in opposite directions from row to row. Join the rows together, making sure to match the seams between the blocks. Add the corner setting triangles last. Trim the outside edges of the quilt top ¼" from the points of the Fan blocks.

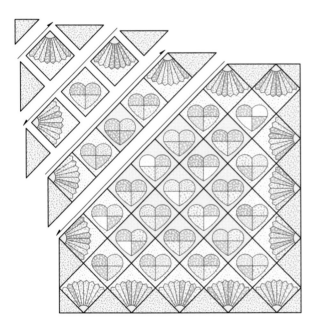

2. Referring to "Straight-Cut Borders" on page 10, measure, trim, and sew the border strips to the side edges of the quilt top first, then to the top and bottom edges. You may leave the borders straight or cut the optional scalloped border as shown in the photo on page 52 (see "Optional Scalloped Border" at right).

   NOTE: *The optional scalloped border is marked before quilting, but not cut.*

3. Layer the quilt top with batting and backing; baste. Quilt as desired.

4. Bind the edges of the quilt. Use bias-grain binding if you make a scalloped border. Add a label.

Optional Scalloped Border

1. Referring to "Making Templates" on page 8, make a template from the scalloped border pattern on page 56. Trace the pattern for the scalloped border onto template plastic, then reverse the pattern, align the center line, and trace the other half to make a complete scallop template. Starting in the middle of a border, place the straight edge of the template along the border seam, with its 2 side edges at the points of 2 Fan blocks.

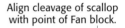
Align cleavage of scallop with point of Fan block.

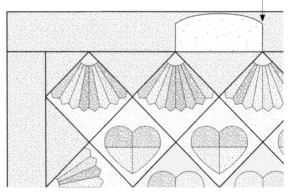

2. Trace around the curved edge of the template; then move the template, again lining up the template's 2 side edges with the points of 2 Fan blocks. Continue tracing scallops until you have 4 scallops on each side of the border. It may be necessary to adjust the scallops due to piecing inaccuracies. Shorten or lengthen the scallops as necessary so that the scallop side edges line up with the points of the Fan blocks.

3. To finish the corners, place the template so that one end lines up with the point of a Fan block and the other end extends beyond the border. Trace the curve to the edge of the border. Place the scallop template on the adjacent corner and repeat.

Smooth out the point where the 2 scallops meet in the corner.

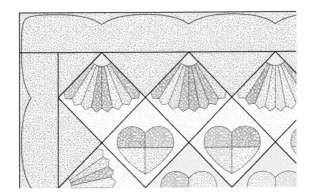

4. Refer to "Bias-Grain Binding" on page 15 to cut bias binding strips. Referring to step 1 of "Straight-Grain Binding" on page 14, piece together a 300"-long strip of binding. Continue as in step 2 on page 14. Then pin the binding to the edges of the quilt, one scallop at a time, following the marked lines. Ease the fullness in the binding to match the marked line; do not stretch the binding. Start along a curved edge of the scallop, rather than at a cleavage point. Stitch the binding in place, stopping at the cleavage point; pivot and then pin the binding to the next scallop. Continue to apply binding in this manner until you reach the starting point.

5. When you reach the beginning of the binding, cut the end 1" longer than needed and tuck the end inside the beginning. Stitch the rest of the binding. Trim excess fabric ¼" from the stitching and trim bulk between scallops. Turn the binding to the back side of the quilt, one scallop at a time. At each cleavage point, turn the binding back on one side of the point and pin, then turn back the binding on the remaining side; a miter will form at the cleavage point. Blindstitch the binding to the back of the quilt. Blindstitch the mitered folds closed, if desired.

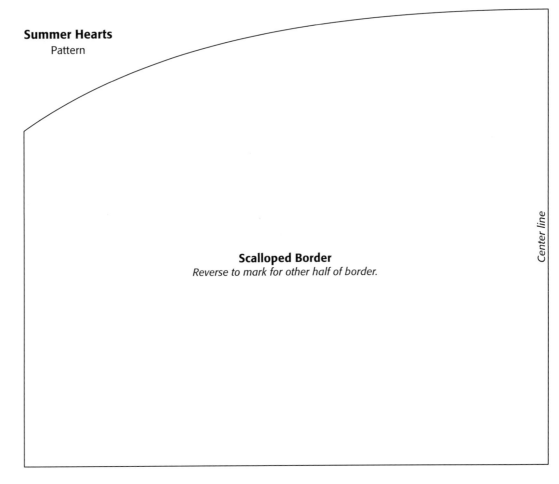

Summer Hearts
Pattern

Scalloped Border
Reverse to mark for other half of border.

Center line

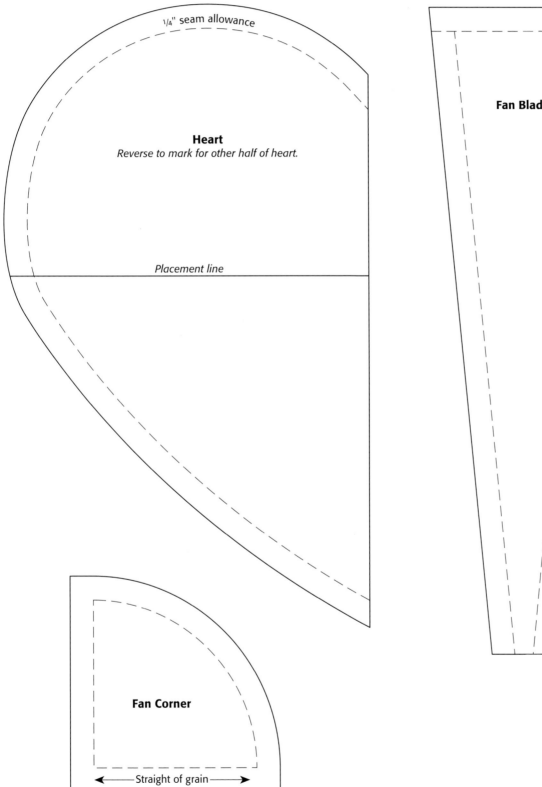

¼" seam allowance

Heart
Reverse to mark for other half of heart.

Placement line

Fan Blade

Fan Corner

← Straight of grain →

Lots of Luvs

Medium pastels are used for the large and small Heart blocks that make up this pretty quilt. The pattern, "Lots of Luvs," is from *Trouble Free Triangles* by Gayle Bong (That Patchwork Place, 1995).

♥

By Cleo Nollette, 2001, Seattle, Washington. Finished quilt size: 53½" x 56½"; finished block size: 9" x 9".

Materials

42"-wide fabric

- ◆ 2 yds. light yellow for background
- ◆ ¾ yd. pale red print for large Heart blocks
- ◆ ½ yd. *total* scraps of light pink, periwinkle, and green for small Heart blocks
- ◆ 1⅛ yds. yellow floral print for border and binding
- ◆ 3⅜ yds. for backing
- ◆ 58" x 61" piece of batting

Cutting Equilateral Triangles and Trapezoids

ALTHOUGH THERE ARE several 60° triangle rulers on the market, they are each marked differently, and they may not all work with the pattern for this quilt. Therefore, we recommend the ClearView Triangle by Sara Nephew. The directions for this project were written with this tool in mind. It allows quick and accurate cutting and comes in three sizes: 6", 8", and 12".

Equilateral Triangles

FOR A drafted equilateral triangle, if you add a ¼" seam allowance to each side, you add ¾" to the triangle's perpendicular measurement, so fabric strips should be cut ¾" wider than the desired finished height of the triangles. Cutting directions for this project indicate the correct width to cut the strips.

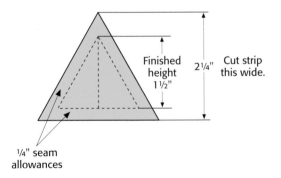

If you are right-handed, begin cutting from the left end of the strip; if you are left-handed, begin from the right end of the strip. For the first cut, place the triangle ruler on the strip, with the left edge of the ruler to one side of the selvage ends. Match the ruled line for the correct-size triangle with the lower edge of the strip. Place the point of the ruler on the upper edge of the strip as shown. Cut on each side of the triangle ruler. For the second cut, rotate the ruler to place its ruled line on the angled cut as shown.

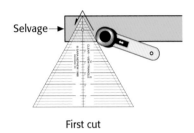

First cut

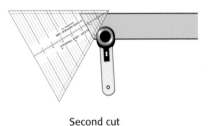

Second cut

Trapezoids

NOTICE THAT a trapezoid is the base of a larger imaginary equilateral triangle (see "Equilateral Triangles" at left). Match the lower edge of the fabric strip with the ruler's mark representing the base of the imaginary cut triangle. Cut on both sides of the triangle ruler as shown. In this example, the strip width is 2", and the height of the imaginary triangle is 9¾".

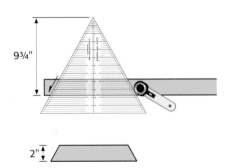

For the next piece, rotate the triangle ruler. Position it to align the mark representing the base of the imaginary cut triangle with the upper edge of the fabric strip. Cut on the right side of the ruler as shown.

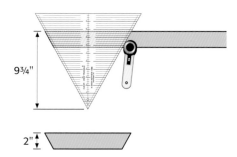

If trapezoids are larger than the base of your triangle ruler, use a combination of rulers butted up against each other to arrive at the proper size and angle. For example, if the height of the imaginary triangle is 9¾" and you need to cut trapezoids from a 2" strip using an 8" ruler, first cut a 60° angle off one end of the strip. Place the triangle ruler 1¾" (9¾" - 8" = 1¾") from the lower edge of the strip. Butt a straight edge against it as shown. Remove the triangle and cut against the straight edge.

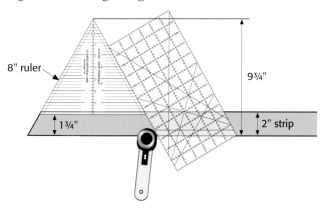

Cutting

NOTE: *All measurements include ¼"-wide seam allowances, unless otherwise indicated. Refer to "Cutting Equilateral Triangles and Trapezoids" on pages 59–60.*

From the light yellow, cut:
- 2 strips, each 2¼" x 42"; from the strips, cut 51 equilateral triangles for background

- 6 strips, each 2" x 42"; from the strips, cut 18 trapezoids with the lower edge of the strip on the ruler's 9¾" mark for background
- 5 strips, each 5¼" x 42"; from the strips, cut 51 equilateral triangles for background
- 3 strips, each 1½" x 42", for background
- 2 strips, each 6" x 42"; from the strips, cut 5 rectangles, each 6" x 10¼". With pairs of rectangles right sides together, cut the rectangles once diagonally to yield 10 side triangles for background.

From the pale red print, cut:
- 2 strips, each 6¾" x 42"; from the strips, cut 18 equilateral triangles for large Heart blocks
- 3 strips, each 2" x 42"; from the strips, cut 36 trapezoids with the lower edge of the strip on the ruler's 3¾" mark for large Heart blocks

From each of the light pink, periwinkle, and green scraps, cut:
- 1 strip, 1¼" x 42", for small Heart blocks
- 1 strip, 3¾" x 42"; from the strip, cut a total of 17 equilateral triangles (8 light pink, 6 periwinkle, and 3 green) for small Heart blocks

From the yellow floral print, cut:
- 6 strips, each 6" x 42", for the border
- 5 strips, each 2½" x 42", for binding

Block Assembly

Large Hearts

1. Sew a 2¼" light yellow triangle to the right side of each pale-red-print trapezoid.

Make 36.

2. Sew these units together in pairs and add a 2¼" light yellow triangle to the left end. Gently press the seams toward the trapezoids.

3. Sew the trapezoid unit to one side of a 6¾" pale-red-print triangle, keeping it on top when you sew, to watch for points. Press seam toward the triangle.

4. Sew a light yellow trapezoid to the top to complete the large Heart blocks. Press gently toward the light trapezoid.

Make 18.

Small Hearts

1. Sew a 1½"-wide light yellow strip to each of the light pink, periwinkle, and green 1¼"-wide strips. Press seams toward the darker strips.

Make 1 each.

2. Cut 2¼" equilateral triangles from the strip sets made in step 1. Use the triangles in which the heart color appears as trapezoids.

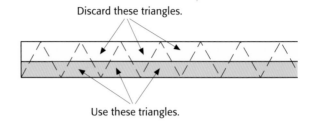

Discard these triangles.

Use these triangles.

2¼"

Cut 16. Cut 12. Cut 6.

3. Sew a 2¼" light yellow equilateral triangle to each of the strip-pieced triangles.

4. Sew the units made in step 3 together in pairs and add a light yellow triangle to the left end. Gently press the trapezoids' seam allowances toward the light yellow triangles.

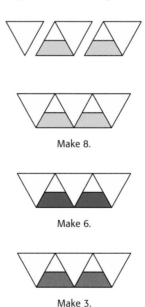

Make 8.

Make 6.

Make 3.

5. Sew the trapezoid unit to a matching 3¾" light pink, periwinkle, or green triangle, keeping it on top when you sew, to watch for points. Press seam toward the large triangle.

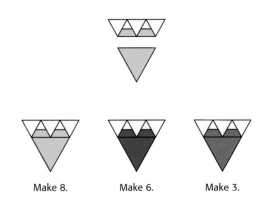

Make 8.   Make 6.   Make 3.

6. Sew a 5¼" light yellow triangle to each side of the small heart, finger-pressing the seam allowances toward the light triangles after sewing each seam. Press.

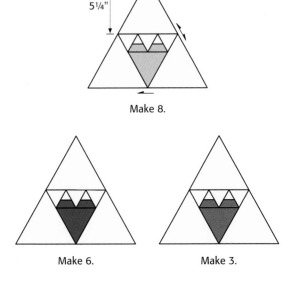

5¼"

Make 8.

Make 6.   Make 3.

Assembly and Finishing

1. Alternating large Heart blocks and small Heart blocks, arrange the blocks into 5 rows as shown. Sew a light yellow side triangle to both ends of each row, as shown. Sew the rows together.

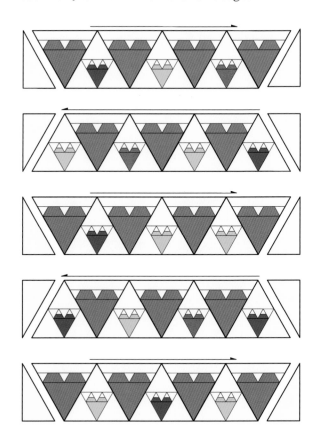

2. Referring to "Straight-Cut Borders" on page 10, measure, trim, and sew the border strips to the side edges of the quilt top, then to the top and bottom edges.

3. Layer the quilt top with batting and backing; baste. Quilt as desired.

4. Bind the edges and add a label.

Petit-Four Hearts

Mint green and ivory hearts with embroidered designs make up this variation on the traditional penny rug.
It has a layer of batting and is quilted with contrasting embroidery floss. Use it as a table topper or wall hanging.
This design is an adaptation of "Petal Hearts," from *Wow! Wool-on-Wool Folk Art Quilts*
by Janet Carija Brandt (That Patchwork Place, 1995).

♥

By Janet Carija Brandt, 2001, Indianapolis, Indiana. Finished quilt size: 32" x 32".

Materials

NOTE: *Dimensions given are for prewashed wool fabric unless otherwise specified (see "Tip" at right). Measurements indicate minimum amounts required for all pieces except the background. Yardage for cotton fabric is based on 42"-wide fabric.*

- ♦ 17" x 17" square off-white wool for hearts
- ♦ 32" x 32" square off-white wool for background
- ♦ 20" x 20" square dark green wool for hearts, flowers, and leaves
- ♦ 17" x 20" rectangle of medium green wool for hearts, flowers, and leaves
- ♦ 17" x17" square light green wool for hearts
- ♦ 1 yd. cotton for backing
- ♦ ½ yd. cotton for bias-grain binding, *or* 2 packages ½"-wide double-fold bias tape
- ♦ 36" x 36" square lightweight batting
- ♦ Contrasting embroidery floss

Cutting

NOTE: *Referring to "Making Templates" on page 8 and using the patterns on page 66, make the heart, flower, and leaf templates. With the templates, trace the required number of designs onto the wool fabrics, using a #2 pencil on light fabrics and a white or yellow pencil on dark fabrics.*

From the off-white wool, cut:
- ♦ 16 hearts

From the dark green wool, cut:
- ♦ 20 hearts
- ♦ 7 flowers
- ♦ 7 leaves

From the medium green wool, cut:
- ♦ 16 hearts
- ♦ 4 flowers
- ♦ 7 leaves

From the light green wool, cut:
- ♦ 16 hearts

Assembly

1. Using 3 strands of embroidery floss, work blanket stitch around all of the hearts (see "Embroidery Stitches" on page 17). Cut the floss long enough to go all the way around a heart without having to change thread. Start with about 40" and adjust as necessary, depending on the size and closeness of your stitches.

   NOTE: *Begin and end the row of blanket stitches at the point of the heart so that no knots show on the reverse of the floppy top "petals" of the hearts.*

Begin and end here.

2. Add embroidered flowers to heart appliqués as indicated in the heart embroidery diagrams on page 66, using the long stitch and the lazy daisy stitch. Also add chain stitching to the heart appliqués. (See "Embroidery Stitches" on page 17.) Do not add running stitches yet.

3. With chalk, pins, or basting thread, mark center lines on the background. Measure and mark 7½" from the outer edge along each line and place the "point" of one off-white heart at each of these marks.

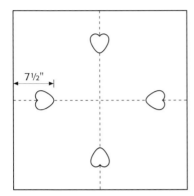

4. Add a dark green heart to each of the 4 corners, 7½" from the outer edge, to finish the first row of hearts. Use a yardstick to check the straightness of the row and to check the distances between hearts as you place them. Pin each heart in the first row with just one pin near its point.

5. Referring to the illustration for color placement, pin the second and third rows of hearts to the background. Pin the third row of hearts so that the point of each heart lies under the second row where 2 hearts touch. It's OK if the tops of the third row's hearts hang over the edge of the background.

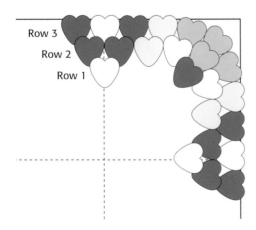

6. Using a running stitch (see "Embroidery Stitches" on page 17), stitch all around the heart appliqués as indicated in the heart embroidery diagrams on page 66, attaching the bottom half of the hearts only to the background at the same time. Pin back the tops of the overlapping hearts as you work.

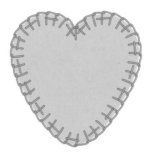

Attach hearts to background
with running stitch.

7. Arrange the center flowers and leaves, following the illustration below or choosing your own arrangement. When you are satisfied with the design, pin and then appliqué the pieces, using a blanket stitch. Embellish the flowers and leaves with a row of chain stitching as indicated on the patterns on page 66.

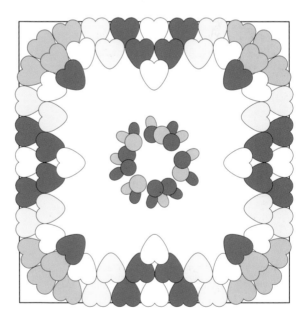

8. Using the embroidery stitches of your choice, initial and date the front of your petal quilt.

Finishing

1. Layer the quilt top with batting and backing; baste. Quilt the center area as desired, using embroidery floss and a running stitch.

2. Leave the corners square or round them off, using a plate or saucer as a guide. Be sure to fold the heart "petals" away from the cutting line.

3. Press the back of the quilt, placing a damp cloth between the quilt and the iron.

4. Bind the edges of the quilt. If you cut the background to make rounded corners, be sure to use bias-grain binding (see page 15) or double-fold bias tape. Take care to ease the binding around the curved edges without stretching it. Add a label.

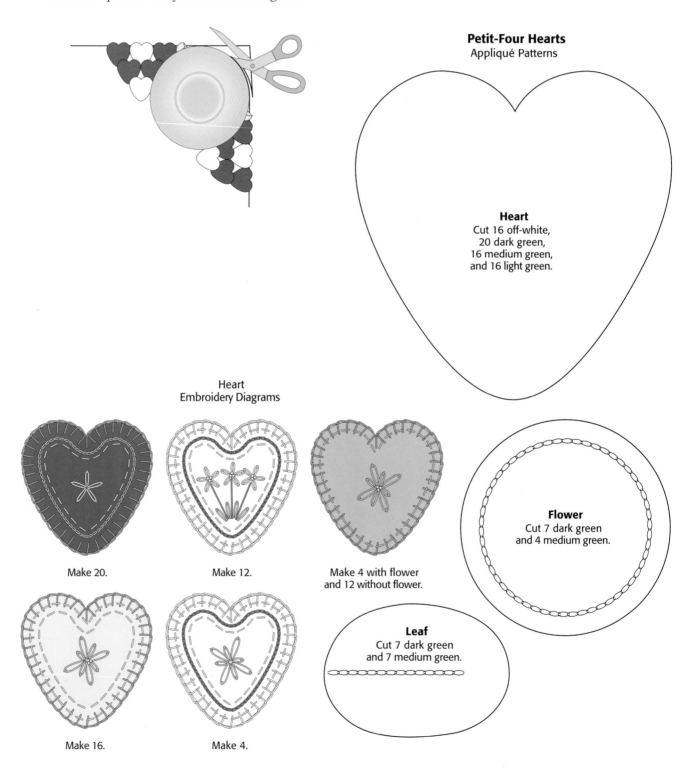

Petit-Four Hearts
Appliqué Patterns

Heart
Cut 16 off-white,
20 dark green,
16 medium green,
and 16 light green.

Heart
Embroidery Diagrams

Make 20.

Make 12.

Make 4 with flower
and 12 without flower.

Make 16.

Make 4.

Flower
Cut 7 dark green
and 4 medium green.

Leaf
Cut 7 dark green
and 7 medium green.

Patchwork Hearts

For this bold trio of hearts, Sandy Bonsib created pieced fabric from 2" squares, then cut the hearts from the fabric and appliquéd them to a background. This design is a new twist on another pieced-heart pattern, "Mosaic Hearts," from Sandy's *Folk Art Quilts* (Martingale & Company, 1998).

♥

By Sandy Bonsib, 2001, Issaquah, Washington. Finished quilt size: 27½" x 48½".

Materials

42"-wide fabric

- ◆ ¼ yd. *total* assorted reds for heart appliqué
- ◆ ¼ yd. *total* assorted yellows for heart appliqué
- ◆ ¼ yd. *total* assorted teals for heart appliqué
- ◆ ⅔ yd. for background
- ◆ ¼ yd. dark red for inner border
- ◆ ⅓ yd. teal for outer border
- ◆ 1½ yds. for backing
- ◆ ⅓ yd. burgundy for binding
- ◆ 32" x 53" piece of batting

Cutting

NOTE: *All measurements include ¼"-wide seam allowances, unless otherwise indicated.*

From the assorted reds, cut:
- ◆ 40 squares, 2" x 2", for heart appliqué

From the assorted yellows, cut:
- ◆ 40 squares, 2" x 2", for heart appliqué

From the assorted teals, cut:
- ◆ 40 squares, 2" x 2", for heart appliqué

From the background fabric, cut:
- ◆ 1 piece, 21" x 42"

From the dark red inner border fabric, cut:
- ◆ 2 strips, each 1½" x 42"
- ◆ 2 strips, each 1½" x 23"

From the teal outer border fabric, cut:
- ◆ 2 strips, each 2½" x 44" (piece the strips as necessary)
- ◆ 2 strips, each 2½" x 27"

From the burgundy, cut:
- ◆ 4 strips, each 2" x 42", for binding

Piecing the Hearts

1. Join 40 assorted squares from each heart color in rows as follows:

   1 row of 3 squares
   2 rows of 4 squares
   1 row of 5 squares
   3 rows of 8 squares

   Press seams in opposite directions from row to row. Join rows as shown.

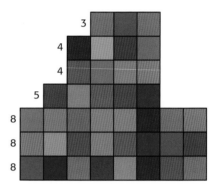

2. Referring to "Basic Appliqué" on page 8 and using the pattern on page 69, make a template and cut 1 heart from each color of pieced squares.

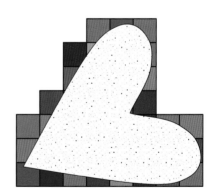

3. Referring to "Needle-Turn Appliqué" on page 8, appliqué your hearts in a vertical row to the center of the background piece, placing the top heart about 5¾" from the upper edge of the background piece and the lower heart about 5" from the lower edge of the background piece (see photograph on page 67 for placement).

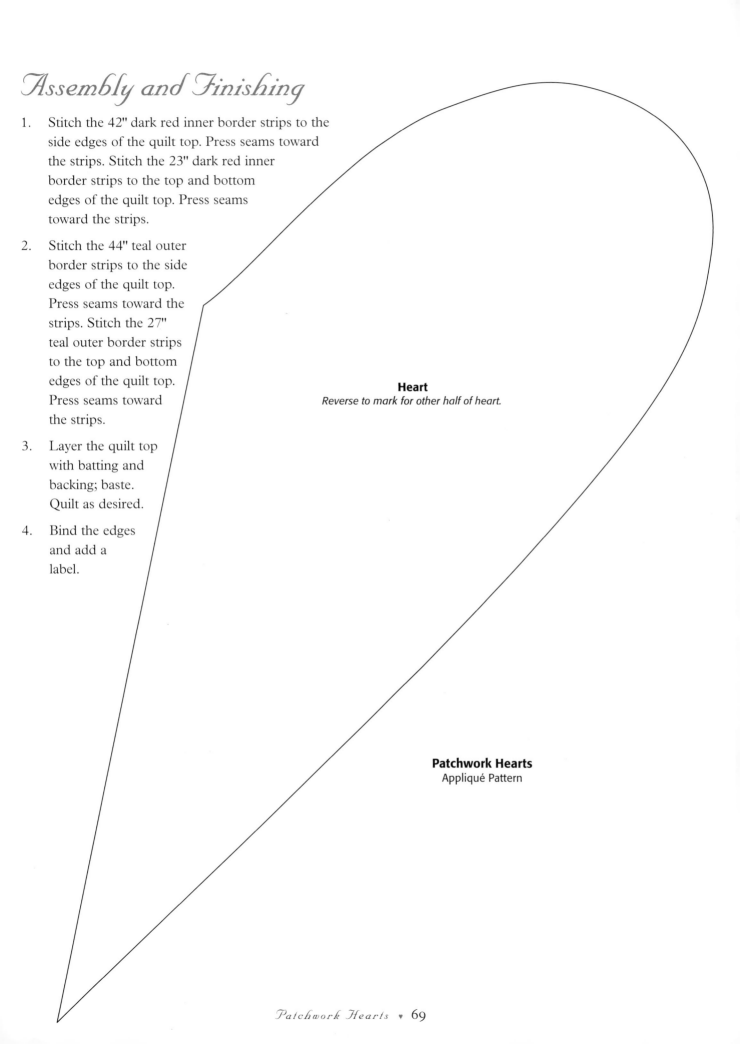

Assembly and Finishing

1. Stitch the 42" dark red inner border strips to the side edges of the quilt top. Press seams toward the strips. Stitch the 23" dark red inner border strips to the top and bottom edges of the quilt top. Press seams toward the strips.

2. Stitch the 44" teal outer border strips to the side edges of the quilt top. Press seams toward the strips. Stitch the 27" teal outer border strips to the top and bottom edges of the quilt top. Press seams toward the strips.

3. Layer the quilt top with batting and backing; baste. Quilt as desired.

4. Bind the edges and add a label.

Heart
Reverse to mark for other half of heart.

Patchwork Hearts
Appliqué Pattern

Soft Summer Roses

This quilt is created from a floral decorator fabric. The design was inspired by "Floral Linen Hearts" in the book *Life in the Country with Country Threads* by Mary Tendall and Connie Tesene (Martingale & Company, 1997).

♥

By Cleo Nollette, 2000, Seattle, Washington. Finished quilt size: 48" x 63"; finished block size: 7¼" x 7¼".

Materials

42"-wide fabric

- ⅝ yd. *total* scraps for heart appliqués
- 3⅝ yds. floral print for blocks and outer border
- ⅜ yd. pink print for flanged inner border
- ½ yd. fabric for binding
- 2⅞ yds. for backing
- 52" x 67" piece of batting

Cutting

NOTE: *All measurements include ¼"-wide seam allowances, unless otherwise indicated.*

From the floral print, cut:

- 35 squares, each 7¾" x 7¾", for blocks
- 2 strips, each 6¼" x 52", from the lengthwise grain of the fabric for the outer border
- 2 strips, each 6¼" x 67", from the lengthwise grain of the fabric for the outer border

From the pink print, cut:

- 5 strips, each 1½" x 42", for the flanged inner border

From the binding fabric, cut:

- 6 strips, each 2" x 42"

Assembly and Finishing

1. Referring to "Basic Appliqué" on page 8 and using the pattern on page 72, make a template and cut 18 hearts from the scraps for heart appliqués, and appliqué each heart to the center of a 7¾" x 7¾" floral print square.

Make 18.

2. Arrange the blocks into 7 rows of 5 blocks each, alternating the appliquéd blocks and the plain floral squares. Sew the blocks into horizontal rows. Join the rows.

3. Referring to step 1 of "Straight-Cut Borders" on page 10, measure and trim the strips for the flanged inner border as for border strips. Fold the strips in half lengthwise; press. Sew the strips to the side edges of the quilt, aligning the long raw edges. Do not press.

4. Referring to step 1 of "Straight-Cut Borders" on page 10, measure and trim the side outer border strips to size. Sew the side outer border strips to the sides of the quilt top, over the flanged inner border, aligning raw edges. Press seam allowances toward the quilt center and press the flange toward the outer border.

5. Referring to step 2 of "Straight-Cut Borders" on page 10, measure and trim the strips for the top and bottom flanged inner border and the top and bottom outer border to size. Fold the flanged inner border strips in half lengthwise; press. Sew the top and bottom flanged inner border strips and outer border strips to the top and bottom of the quilt in the same manner as for the sides. Press the seam allowances toward the quilt center and press the flange toward the outer border.

6. Layer the quilt top with batting and backing; baste. Quilt as desired.

7. Bind the edges and add a label.

Soft Summer Roses
Appliqué Pattern

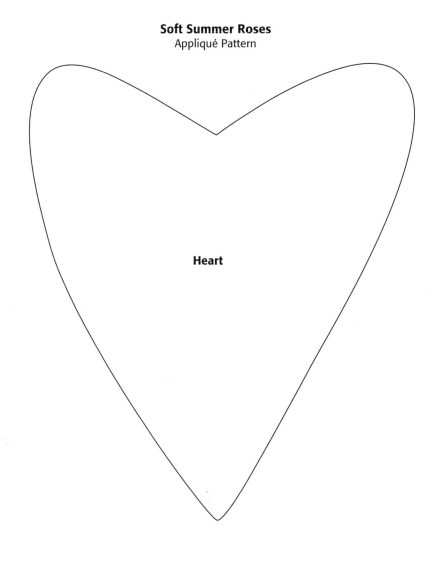

Heart

A Blue and Yellow Basket

A generous basket holds an exuberant bouquet of flowers. Use needle-turn appliqué,
or try the all-machine appliqué technique described on the following pages. For a really quick alternative,
skip the basket and make the whole quilt with Heart and Chain blocks.

♥

By Mary Hickey, 2001, Seattle, Washington. Finished quilt size: 38½" x 44½";
finished block sizes: Heart block, 6" x 6", Chain block, 6" x 6", basket section, 18" x 18".

Materials

42"-wide fabric

♦ 1⅛ yds. white for background
♦ 1½ yds. *total* assorted medium blues for Heart blocks, morning-glory and leaf appliqués, basket trim, basket handle, outer border, and binding
♦ ½ yd. *total* assorted golds and yellows for corners of Heart blocks, four-patch units in Chain blocks, basket trim, and tulip appliqués
♦ ¼ yd. pale-blue-and-white print for four-patch units in Chain blocks
♦ ½ yd. *total* assorted light blues for center squares in Chain blocks, border around basket section, inner border, and stem and leaf appliqués
♦ ¼ yd. blue check for basket
♦ ⅜ yd. large floral print for setting triangles around basket
♦ ⅛ yd. or scraps of golden brown for tulip appliqués
♦ 1½ yds. fabric for backing
♦ 43" x 49" piece of batting
♦ ¼ yd. lightweight Pellon interfacing
♦ 2 white and 2 yellow buttons
♦ ⅓" and ½" bias bars
♦ Water-soluble pen

Cutting

NOTE: *All measurements include ¼"-wide seam allowances, unless otherwise indicated.*

From the white, cut:

♦ 4 strips, each 1½" x 42"; crosscut 2 of the strips into 40 squares, each 1½" x 1½", for background in Heart blocks; crosscut 2 of the strips into 10 rectangles, each 1½" x 6½", for background in Heart blocks
♦ 2 strips, each 3½" x 42"; crosscut the strips into 20 squares, each 3½" x 3½", for background in Heart blocks
♦ 3 strips, each 2½" x 42"; crosscut the strips into 44 squares, each 2½" x 2½", for background in Chain blocks

♦ 1 square, 12½" x 12½"; cut the square once diagonally to yield 2 triangles. One triangle will be used for the top half of the basket section and the other will be cut into small pieces for the bottom half of the section.

From assorted medium blues, cut:

♦ 2 strips, each 5½" x 42"; crosscut the strips into 20 rectangles, each 3½" x 5½", cutting an even number of rectangles from each fabric for the Heart blocks
♦ 5 strips, each 3½" x 42", for outer border
♦ 1 strip, 1½" x 42"; cut the strip in half to make 2 strips, each 1½" x 21", for the basket trim
♦ 5 strips, each 2" x 42", for binding
    Set aside the remaining medium blues for the morning-glory, leaf, and basket-handle appliqués

From the assorted golds and yellows, cut:

♦ 4 strips, each 1½" x 42"; cut 1 of the strips in half to make 2 strips, each 1½" x 21"; use 1 short strip for the basket trim and the remaining strips for the four-patch units in the Chain blocks
♦ 2 strips, each 1½" x 42"; crosscut the strips into 40 squares, each 1½" x 1½", for the corners of the Heart blocks

From the pale-blue-and-white print, cut:

♦ 4 strips, each 1½" x 42"; cut 1 of the strips in half to make 2 strips, each 1½" x 21", for four-patch units in Chain blocks. (Only 1 of the 1½" x 21" strips will be used.)

From the assorted light blues, cut:

♦ 2 strips, each 1" x 42"; crosscut the strips into 2 pieces, each 1" x 12½", and 2 pieces, each 1" x 13", for the border around the basket section
♦ 4 strips, each 1½" x 42", for the inner border
♦ 1 strip, 2½" x 42"; crosscut the strip into 11 squares, each 2½" x 2½", for the centers of the Chain blocks
    Set aside the remaining light blues for the stem and leaf appliqués.

From the large floral print, cut:

♦ 2 squares, each 11" x 11"; cut the squares once diagonally to yield 4 setting triangles to surround basket section. (They will be slightly larger than needed; you will trim them later.)

Heart Block Assembly

1. Use a pencil to draw a light diagonal line on the back of the 40 white 1½" squares and 20 white 3½" squares.

2. Place the squares on the medium blue rectangles and stitch as shown to make 10 right halves and 10 left halves for the heart units. For each heart unit, use the same medium blue fabric for each half of the unit. Trim ¼" from the stitching lines and press seam allowances toward the darker fabric.

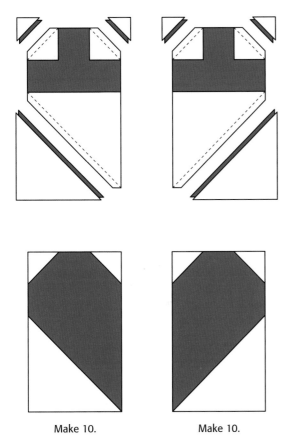

Make 10.　　　Make 10.

3. Stitch the right and left halves of the hearts together to complete the heart units.

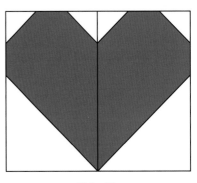

Make 10.

4. Use a pencil to draw a light diagonal line on the back of the 40 gold 1½" squares. Place a square at each end of a 1½" x 6½" white rectangle, right sides together, and stitch on the drawn lines. Trim ¼" from the stitching lines and press seam allowances toward the darker fabric. The remaining gold squares will be used in step 6.

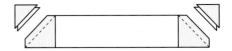

5. Stitch the pieced unit from step 4 to the upper edge of the heart unit from step 3 as shown.

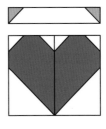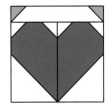

Make 10.

6. Place a gold square in both lower corners of the heart unit, right sides together. Stitch on the drawn lines. Trim ¼" from the stitching lines and press seam allowances toward the darker fabric.

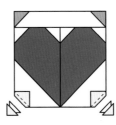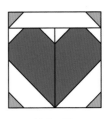

Make 10.

Chain Block Assembly

1. Join the 1½" pale-blue-and-white print strips to the 1½" yellow strips. Crosscut the strips into 88 segments, 1½" wide. Join 2 segments together as shown to make a four-patch unit.

 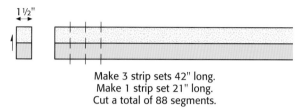

Make 3 strip sets 42" long.
Make 1 strip set 21" long.
Cut a total of 88 segments.

Make 44.

2. Join the 2½" white squares, the 2½" light blue squares, and the four-patch units into rows as shown. Join the rows together to make a Chain block.

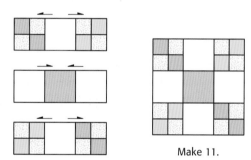

Make 11.

Basket Section Assembly

1. Join the 1½" x 21" yellow and medium blue strips as shown. Crosscut the unit into 1½" segments.

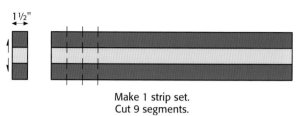

Make 1 strip set.
Cut 9 segments.

2. Tilt the segments on point and stitch them together, matching the points where the yellow corners meet.

3. Referring to "Making Templates" on page 8 and using the patterns on pages 79–80, make templates 1–4, including seam allowances as indicated on patterns. For templates 1 and 2, trace the pattern onto template plastic, then reverse pattern, align center line, and trace the other half to complete the templates. Position template 2 on the strip of squares with the center line of the template centered through one yellow square. Cut around the template to create the band that goes across the top of the basket.

4. From the blue check fabric, cut a template 1 piece for the base of the basket. Stitch the band to the top of the basket, with the band piece on top, being careful to sew next to, but not on top of, the points of the yellow squares.

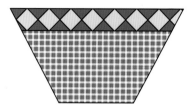

5. From 1 of the 2 large white triangles, cut templates 3 and 4. Sew the long, thin triangles to the sides of the basket, and stitch the small triangle to the bottom of the basket. Stitch the remaining large triangle to the top of the basket.

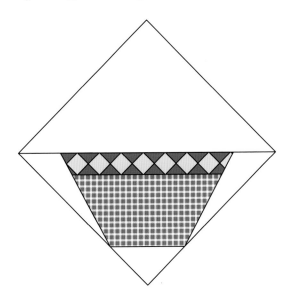

6. Sew the 1" x 12½" light blue border strips to opposite sides of the basket section. Sew the 1" x 13" strips to the remaining 2 sides of the section. Press the seams toward the border.

7. Sew the large floral print setting triangles to the basket section. Trim to make an 18½" square.

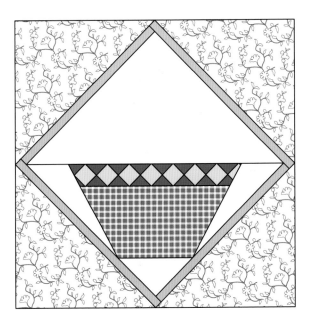

Appliqué the Basket Handle and Flowers

NOTE: *The instructions below are for machine appliqué. If you prefer, you can appliqué the pieces by hand (see "Needle-Turn Appliqué" on page 8). To create a smooth basket handle and graceful flower stems, use metal or plastic bias bars available at quilt shops and fabric stores.*

Handle and Flower Stems

1. Cut 1 bias strip of medium blue fabric 1½" x 18" for the basket handle and 4 bias strips of light blue fabric 1¼" x 18" for the flower stems. Fold each strip in half wrong sides together and press. Stitch ⅛" from the raw edges.

2. Insert a bias bar into a fabric tube, using a ½" bar for the basket handle and a ⅓" bar for the stems. Twist the bar to bring the seam to the center of one of the flat sides of the bar. Press the seam flat with an iron. Remove the bar. Repeat for all fabric tubes.

3. Position the handle on the basket section and carefully pin it in place as shown on the appliqué placement guide on page 78. Using a narrow zigzag stitch and thread matching the handle fabric, stitch the handle to the basket section.

4. Cut the stem tubes to the desired lengths and position the stems on the block, using the appliqué placement guide on page 78; pin in place. Stitch the stems in place as for the basket handle.

Flowers and Leaves

1. Using the patterns on page 80 and a water-soluble pen, trace 8 tulips, 2 of each morning glory, 4 morning-glory flower bases, and 6 leaves onto Pellon interfacing. Cut out the shapes, allowing ¼" for seam allowances.

2. Place a Pellon morning-glory flower on the right side of a medium blue flower fabric and stitch along the traced line, using a small stitch length. Carefully trim away the excess fabric, leaving only a scant ⅛" seam allowance.

3. Cut a slit about 1¼" long through the white Pellon interfacing only. Spray the flower lightly with water and turn right side out. The spray removes the water-soluble pen lines and helps create a smooth edge. Use the end of a chopstick to smooth the arcs and curves of the flower. Make 3 additional morning-glory flowers, 4 morning-glory flower bases, and 6 leaves in the same manner, using assorted medium blue fabrics. Make 8 tulips, using assorted gold, yellow, and golden brown fabrics.

4. Position the flowers, flower bases, and leaves on the block and carefully pin them in place as shown on the appliqué placement guide below. Stitch in place as for the basket handle and stems.

5. Stitch buttons to the centers of the morning-glory flowers.

Appliqué Placement Guide

Assembly and Finishing

1. Arrange the Heart and Chain blocks and the basket section as shown. Join the top row of blocks. Join the blocks in the bottom 2 rows.

2. Join the side blocks to make 2 vertical columns. Stitch the columns to the sides of the basket section.

3. Join the top row and the 2 bottom rows of blocks to the basket section.

4. Referring to "Borders with Mitered Corners" on page 11, measure the quilt top for mitered borders. Join the light blue strips to the medium blue strips and treat them as one. Sew the combined border strips to the quilt, mitering the corners.

5. Layer the quilt with batting and backing: baste. Quilt as desired.

6. Bind the edges and add a label.

A Blue and Yellow Basket
Patterns

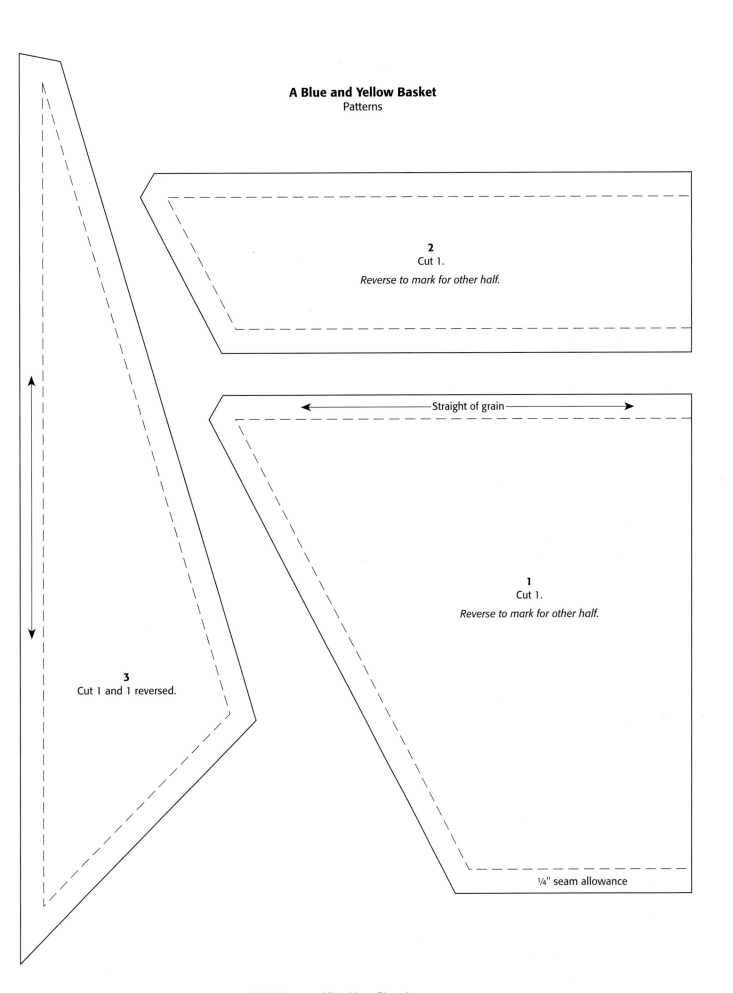

2
Cut 1.

Reverse to mark for other half.

Straight of grain

1
Cut 1.

Reverse to mark for other half.

3
Cut 1 and 1 reversed.

¼" seam allowance

A Blue and Yellow Basket
Patterns

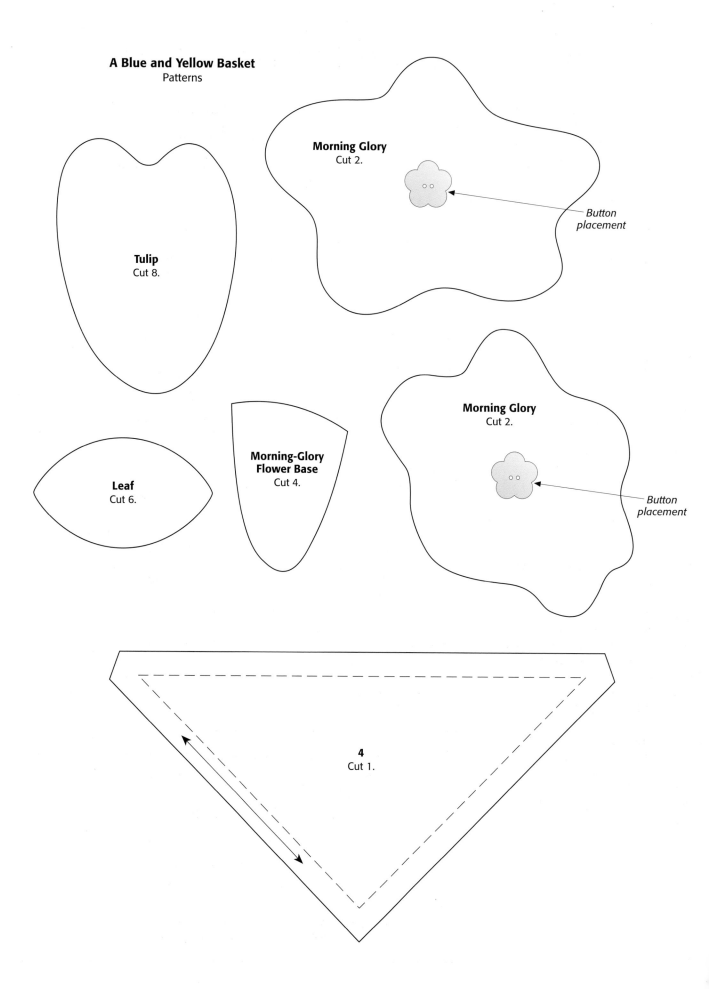

Tulip
Cut 8.

Morning Glory
Cut 2.

Button placement

Leaf
Cut 6.

Morning-Glory Flower Base
Cut 4.

Morning Glory
Cut 2.

Button placement

4
Cut 1.